better
TOGETHER

Discovering the Dynamic Results
of Cooperation

Paul Fleischmann

HigherLife Publishing & Marketing, Inc.
Oviedo, FL

better
TOGETHER

Discovering the Dynamic Results
of Cooperation

Paul Fleischmann

ISBN: 978-1-939183-65-1 Paperback

14 15 16 17 – 9 8 7 6 5 4 3 2 1
Printed in the United States of America.

DEDICATION

To those who have poured into my life so deeply and so consistently,
those with whom I am so much "Better Together."

My wife Toni,
Dan Maltby, now with Jesus,
Carson Kiesel, my accountability partner and faithful friend.

ENDORSEMENTS

The times we live in mandate networking as a necessity, not an option. *Better Together* is a rare treasure of wisdom and experience that will help us work together to reach our world.

— Josh McDowell
Founder, Josh McDowell Ministries

Linking arms with Paul has been one of the great privileges of my life! From the National Network's beginning we have learned and lived out the values of *Better Together*. I can attest that every story and the principles behind them have the mark of proven reality.

— Barry St. Clair
President, Reach Out Youth Solutions

Our cities are fragmented. The message of *Better Together* is desperately needed to connect urban leaders and ministries in order to more effectively reach this young and urban world.

— Larry Acosta
Urban Youth Worker Institute

Whether applied to youth or adults, the principles outlined in *Better Together* pave the pathway to spiritual impact. Paul discipled me when I was in high school, and I know first-hand the effectiveness of his insights,   teaching, and ministry. You are in for a blessing.

— Randy Pope
Senior Pastor, Perimeter Church

Paul Fleischmann's *Better Together* is an inspiring and practical road map to help you achieve Spirit-empowered unity in your ministry, vocation, and even your personal relationships.

— Ron Boehme
Youth with a Mission

God raises up people and movements to lead the way for each specific generation. *Better Together* is an inspiring story of how God used grassroots networking across America and around the world to bring about spiritual renewal among young people. This book reads like a beautiful story.

— Jim Burns
President, HomeWord

Teamwork works. *Better Together* tells impacting stories of how teamwork helped ministries fulfill their purposes and goals over several decades. Readers will feel the urge to impact today's culture by revealing God's love—but they will realize it is most likely to happen if they choose to not travel alone.

— Chris Maxwell
Director of Spiritual Life, Emmanuel College

"Paul Fleischmann has spent the better part of his life living out the heartbeat of *Better Together*. I can't think of anyone better to rally the church around our common cause of bringing the gospel to every person possible. The principles in this book are counter-culture to most norms, but will bring anyone willing into a broader Jesus-coalition with greater impact than any of us could have on our own. Hopefully, we will all gladly give in to the glorious reality that we is greater than me."

— Louie Giglio
Passion City Church, Atlanta

ACKNOWLEDGMENTS

There is no way to thank everyone who has contributed to the process of creating *Better Together*. At the risk of overlooking some, I am counting on the premise asserted in this book that all of us have left our "logos and egos at the door!" My heart-felt thanks to all of you!

Daryl Nuss – my chief advisor and right-hand man on the book. His memory goes back as far as mine, but he remembers things I have forgotten or didn't know.

Our Wives – who supported us in countless ways: **Donna Nuss,** Daryl's wife, headed up a staff prayer effort every week. **Toni Fleischmann,** my wife, understood the significance of this project to me and was extremely patient, despite her "distracted" husband. Both Donna and Toni had invaluable perspectives, ideas, and suggestions that made their way into the book.

Barry St. Clair – a life-long friend whom I discovered "pre-Network" at our first meeting in 1979. He walked by my side then, helping to craft the Network Covenant and Objectives, and he has continued to this day by helping me to tell the story of what God has done since the formation of the Network. We have experienced first-hand what it means to be *Better Together* through challenging times in personal life and ministry. His experience as an author and his ready availability were invaluable to me.

Better Together Teams

In a book about networking it makes sense that there would be "teams" of people collaborating and contributing to make the project happen.

Ministry Sponsors – Possibly, the most unique aspect of this book is that it has been a joint project of like-minded ministries from day one. While it was just an idea, key donors came behind it. Before a word was written, fellow youth ministries agreed to sponsor and co-brand the book to make it a resource for networking and collaboration in their own ministries. To the sponsors listed in this book: "From the bottom of my heart, thank you for believing in me and for your deep commitment to networking our efforts in the cause of Christ."

Reading Team – Thank you to the team of readers who were my "sanity check" on each chapter: Doug Clark, Doug Tegner, Ron Boehme, Daryl and Donna Nuss, Toni Fleischmann, and Barry St. Clair. Special thanks go to Dr. Dale Taliaferro who critiqued and advised my many Scripture references throughout the book. Refining the content was a rich blessing for me.

Focus Groups – My thanks to the Network's Regional Coordinators who conceived of a book like this apart from any dream of mine. They gave valuable input as to the concepts, principles, and use of *Better Together* among our 800 local youth worker networks. At the design level, many thanks to people I didn't even meet who offered their opinions on the cover design and graphics.

Office Team – In particular, thanks to Mark Stephens, the Network's director of operations. He has been the "glue" for so many NNYM projects as he has been for this book. Mark has been a constant help to me – for financial processes, graphic work, and selfless service in whatever way possible.

Prayer Teams – Thanks to the many on our personal support team and our "Prayer Hotline" who consistently undergirded this project with their prayers and even financial support.

Publishing Team – It has been a pleasure to work with HigherLife Publishing and all of their fine staff, including the copy editors, designer, and our Project Manager Pamela Wisner. President David Welday was a personal inspiration and mentor in urging me to move forward with my vision to address the topics stirring within me, and this book in particular.

TABLE OF CONTENTS

FOREWORD

"Help! My four-year-old daughter is lost in the cornfield!" My attention was immediately riveted to this news story.

I was raised on a farm in the Midwest and know how easy it is to lose a small child among the tall corn stalks. The mother had reason to panic. The cornfield was 152 acres. It was five o'clock on a hot and windy summer afternoon. The article reported that 284 people and a helicopter searched frantically until eleven o'clock that night. Though tempted to break until daylight, the fear for her safety drove them to conduct one more search.

This time the county sheriff took a different approach. He formed everyone into lines, instructing them to move together methodically. Providentially, within minutes someone's flashlight reflected on the little girl's white tee shirt. She was safe. Her mother and volunteers sobbed with joy and relief. The article said they were "amazed at what they had seen as this rural area came together."[1]

My Experience

This story resonated with me because it underscores how we are at our best when we work together. When there is something we really care about, when we are facing an urgent situation, we shouldn't just run around frantically. We shouldn't remain independent of others if we expect to solve a challenging issue.

I'm passionate about this book because, while it draws on insights from past experiences, it also reveals principles that will be valuable for anyone who wants to network more effectively in the future. This is what we have discovered in the National Network of Youth Ministries over and over—we are "better together."

The Author

As you will discern in the following pages, Paul Fleischmann is the perfect person to write this book. Paul served as the president of the National Network of Youth Ministries for almost thirty years. His experience suited him to serve on boards of other networks like the National Association of Evangelicals, Mission America Coalition, World Evangelical Alliance Youth Commission, and the National Prayer Committee.

The principles of networking are not theory to Paul. They have been forged on the anvil of passion, experience, and reality.

It has been a pleasure to be one of Paul's sounding boards for the development of this book.

Principles Apply Broadly

My guess is that you are holding this book in your hands because you want to learn more about how God can maximize your efforts in doing ministry together. Although many of the insights and stories come from our youth ministry experience, this book is intended to bring insight to any collaborative, ministry effort. For example:

- If you are involved in *Ministry* – serving youth or in any other area of giftedness or passion
- If you are a *Christian leader* – motivated to connect with other like-minded leaders
- If you are a *student leader* – wanting to make an impact on

your campus or community

• If you are a *concerned adult* – parent, educator, social worker, or marketplace leader and desire to see greater impact through your involvement with children, youth, and other segments of our society

Whatever your position or perspective, I encourage you to join others in coming to a better understanding through this book of the dynamic results of cooperation.

Benefits Go Deep

It is our heart's desire that the concepts and challenges of *Better Together* will encourage us to work together as never before. As you read the book, the benefits will become obvious. But I've discovered that the values of networking are not only about ministry results. As we learn to humbly work together with those of diverse gifts and backgrounds, we come to understand things about God's essence and character that can only be discerned in unity (John 17:21-22). It's exciting to see networking not only has an impact upon others but also upon our own personal relationship with God.

It is my prayer that the Lord will speak to each of our hearts and minds as we unpack the principles and insights in *Better Together*.

Daryl Nuss
Executive Director/CEO
National Network of Youth Ministries
San Diego, CA

INTRODUCTION

"May they experience such perfect unity
that the world will know that You sent Me
and that You love them as much as you love Me"
(John 17:23b, NLT).

I t's a mystery to me that in God's grand design for the universe He repeatedly chooses to demonstrate His attributes through partnership with people like you and me. Of course, the greatest example of God's commitment to relationship with us is the sacrifice of His only Son Jesus to redeem all who believe in Him as our Savior from sin. Envisioning God's compassion to seek and save the lost (Luke 19:10) continues to draw my heart to Him in gratitude.

What compels me even further is to see Jesus' actual conversation about us with His Father during His final earthly hours. In John 17, Jesus earnestly prayed for all of us to experience the same love His Father has for Him (v. 23), to know God the Father *personally* and *eternally* (v. 3), and to live in a relationship that offers His protection (vv. 11, 15), joy (v. 13), holiness (vv. 17, 19), and glory (v. 22).

And, Jesus wanted us to be His partners in the greatest cause of all time – spreading His Father's love through the gospel to every person everywhere (John 17:23, Matthew 28:18-20).

Another part of the mystery for me is the way Jesus said this mission would be accomplished – not by programs, power, or politics. *Jesus indicated that the world will believe our message when we come together in complete unity* – *both with God and with each other* (John 17:21-23). How is that possible? It brings to mind what God said to the prophet in Zechariah 4:6: "Not by might, nor by power, but by my Spirit, says the Lord Almighty."

In the 1970s some of us observed that God was motivating youth ministries, more than ever before, to work together in unity. For instance, in 1971 some of the largest parachurch, youth organizations responded to conflicts between local campus chapters by crafting the Trail West Agreement – a commitment (still ongoing) to unity, coordination, communication, and mutual support.

There were other stirrings of God drawing people together. Youth ministries began to become more aware of duplication and common concerns. One of the results was that God laid it on the hearts of twenty-five youth ministry leaders from twenty-one different ministries to meet together. On January 8-10, 1979, a "Forum on Youth Discipleship" was held at Christ Haven Lodge in Florissant, Colorado, in the heart of the Rocky Mountains. It was the first of many such meetings and eventually became the catalyst that initiated the formation of the National Network of Youth Ministries in 1981.

The Network (as it will be referred to in this book) became a coalition of youth ministries committed to a common goal of reaching and discipling teenagers in every community for Christ. The Network serves to unite local youth workers and national ministries. Church youth pastors, parachurch workers, teachers, and other caring adults are united through prayer, relationships, strategy, and resources.

Locally, there are now over 800 youth ministry networks, representing every state, and involving over 100,000 youth workers. More than 1,200 regional, state, and local Network coordinators give leadership to these networks. The Network is probably best known for See You At The

Pole and the National Student Day of Prayer, which rallies one to two million students annually to pray for their schools, their friends, and their nation.

Nationally, there are approximately 150 youth ministry organizations that are associated with the Network. These organizations recognize that the vision to reach and disciple every teenager cannot be accomplished unless we work together. Approximately 250,000 youth workers make up the staffs of those ministries, representing about 100,000 churches and three million youth. Since 1990 many of the top executive leaders of these national ministries meet together annually at an event called the Youth Ministry Executive Council.

Internationally, the Network has been connected in fifty other countries with sister networks that are also seeking to reach their nation's youth for Christ. In a variety of settings, they serve as resources and consultants.

It has been remarkable to observe God at work all these years – drawing leaders with differing opinions, gifts, and personalities to a place of shared values and goals. As a founder, CEO, and now president emeritus of the Network, I feel it is our stewardship responsibility to lift up what God has done and to share the principles, lessons, and convictions He has shown us. The motivation is not to tell the history of the Network, although Network history is often the source of examples. Rather, this book is designed to serve the body of Christ in the future. Its intention is to show what our experiences have revealed and what we believe may be of value to anyone who wants to multiply their impact through cooperation.

Better Together tells the story of what happens when leaders are willing to set aside their logos and egos in order to unite for a cause. The book highlights twelve universal networking principles, demonstrated to be essential and effective based on examples of the Network and its partners. Though many of the illustrations are from youth ministry, care has been taken to select principles that are applicable and helpful to anyone who wants to network. The principles are simple. In fact, for a quick summary of the twelve principles just refer to the Table of Contents. Each chapter will explain the principle, give examples with Scripture, and suggest questions for how the principles can be practically applied. (Note that the sub-heads in each chapter outline the key elements of the chapter's principle.)

It might be good to pause here to clarify what I mean by "networking." When the National Network of Youth Ministries was founded in 1981, the term "network" had very few of the connotations that it does today. Now the term is so used, misused, and muddied that, for some, "networking" is just a nonessential time of fellowship. For others, who feel they have tried it without success, it is an overrated, idealistic attempt to accomplish something together that could have been easier to accomplish alone.

The standard definition of "networking" is to share information, services, and contacts in an area of common interest. For the National Network of Youth Ministries, these are a valid part of networking, but they are just the beginning – the entry-level, one track of a multi-track process. From the beginning, the Network's cornerstone was more than just *common interest.* It was *common conviction* about the urgent need to reach teenagers for Christ – a conviction that facilitated openness between groups unaccustomed to working together (like Baptists and Pentecostals) in order to aid them in finding common ground. We experienced networking as a process which starts with *connection*, grows into *cooperation*, enables *coordination*, and finally steps up to *collaboration*. (More about this in Chapter 5: ***Mutual Trust***.)

At the time of this writing the southwestern states have been   rampant with wildfires. Firefighters from many cities have joined forces to battle the blazes. For them to network in the traditional sense of the word – sharing about resources and contacts – might have been a necessary first step, but it would have been wholly inadequate to stop the fires. The blazing infernos, devouring thousands of acres, many homes, and human lives, demand more than *connection*. The critical needs instill an urgency within those involved. Those critical needs drive them to step up their networking efforts to levels which produce *cooperation, coordination,* and *collaboration.* By working together, they can win a battle that no one firefighter or agency could do alone.

In this book, we will examine the stories and principles that led to the kind of unity that God blessed, producing far-reaching results. If some see this book as an apologetic for networking, it will be one based on experiences, not arguments. Look for the themes that emerge: humility, servant-leadership, listening, spiritual power, and God's use of small things and ordinary people.

I invite you to join me on this journey down a path where God's footprints and signposts are everywhere. My prayer is that we will learn from the past so that the next generation can continue God's work in the future – even as the Psalmist urged us to do in Psalm 78:2-4, 7.

> I will open my mouth in parables;
> I will utter hidden things, things from of old—
> what we have heard and known,
> what our fathers have told us.
> We will not hide them from their children;
> we will tell the next generation
> the praiseworthy deeds of the Lord,
> His power, and the wonders He has done.
> Then they would put their trust in God
> and would not forget His deeds
> but would keep His commands.

The stories, principles, and applications in this book are meant to help us faithfully remember God's "praiseworthy deeds" (v. 4) in order that we can "put our trust in God" (v. 7) for the challenges of the future.

Chapter 1

PASSIONATE VISION

I was just 15 years old, a sophomore at Marshall High School in Portland, Oregon. As president of my campus Youth for Christ Club, I had the chance to go to a city-wide training with all the other school club officers. Willie Foote, our YFC staff leader, made a statement I will never forget, "If you don't reach your school for Christ, no one else will!"

All the way home, those words echoed in my head. The first moment I was alone, I fell to my knees, praying for our club, my friends, and the many who weren't Christians at my school.

"But Lord," I prayed, "there are over 2,200 kids on my campus . . . and I'm only in tenth grade! I've never done anything like this before. I don't know what I'm doing!"

I began to weep for the first time over kids without Christ. I really wanted the Lord to use me, but it all seemed so overwhelming. Over the next three years God did use me, along with other fellow leaders, to reach out to hundreds of students at my school. Many of our classmates came to Christ, and some are in ministry today.

But I didn't know that then.

Driven by a Compelling Need

Fast-forward eighteen years to a group of twenty-five adult leaders on their knees weeping together over similar groups of kids that did not know Christ. They were leaders of twenty-one different ministries, hand-picked from across the country. They spent three days at a mountain retreat in the Colorado Rockies, getting acquainted, sharing what was going on in their ministries, and evaluating how they were doing overall in reaching our nation's teenagers for Christ. They were just as over-whelmed as I had been as a teenager. Everyone agreed that we were falling far short of what needed to be done to even make a dent in reaching the millions of young people who were without Christ.

It was 1979. Teenagers were entering the "me generation." They were self-focused, fearful, and fragmented. There weren't nearly enough youth workers, and most of those trying to serve were not staying very long – an average of twelve to eighteen months. Competition between ministries and churches was the elephant in the room. Duplication of ministry efforts was shocking.

> Competition between ministries and churches was the elephant in the room. Duplication of ministry efforts was shocking.

Sure, each ministry had a unique brand and style; each was effective in its own way. But this sobering truth began to grip them: despite all the efforts of many organizations, the vast majority of teenagers were not being reached or discipled. These leaders talked and prayed in pairs and small clusters – for some, late into the night.

They started to get a glimpse outside the walls of their own ministries, a glimpse that gave them a fresh perspective and a broader understanding of the youth culture. Encouraged by how much they had in common, these leaders began to build relationships. Some started thinking about how much more could be done if they worked together.

When they gathered as a group, some wept as their shared burden for reaching this lost generation drove them to their knees. They asked

God to spawn a movement of His Spirit among youth in America.

Yes, these strong leaders had their differences. But the compelling need to reach teenagers for Christ had begun to draw them together. What was intended to be a one-time gathering ignited a joint vision that motivated them to think beyond their differences. Two years later in 1981, that vision gave birth to the National Network of Youth Ministries.

Cru (known then as Campus Crusade for Christ) hosted this first Forum, providing lodging and meals. Roger Randall, the director of Cru's high school ministry, shares his memory of what happened. "What a GOD thing. I felt the Lord gave us three things in that original Forum:

> • **Common Vision** – the fervent desire to reach every teenager in America.
>
> • **Common Philosophy** – the need to be culturally relevant in our evangelism and discipleship.
>
> • **Uncommon Camaraderie** – The glue of the Network would not be common tools or training but loving and ministering to one another. We knew all too well the challenges in the lives of youth workers and that they often have no one with whom to share their needs. We could speak to one another as peers and call one another to effectiveness and godliness."[2]

The Passion Behind the Vision

"The kingdom of heaven is like treasure hidden in a field . . . in his joy, he went and sold all he had and bought that field" (Matthew 13:44).

Many people have a vision, but passion is what gives the vision power. Passion is what makes your vision compelling and captivating, like the man who found the treasure in the field. He was so full of joy about what he had found that he was overcome with urgency to make it his, gladly investing everything he had. Rick Warren, pastor of Saddleback Church, said: "Nothing great is ever accomplished in life without passion. Passion is what energizes life. Passion makes the impossible possible." [3]

> Nothing great is ever accomplished in life without passion. Passion makes the impossible possible.

From the very beginning of the Network, the deep burden to reach the emerging generation has been a common cause that motivates leaders to work together. Today, youth workers are still passionate about that cause. In fact, the cause is even more pronounced due to the complexity of today's cultural impact on forty-two million youth, ages ten to nineteen.[4] These are the future leaders of our families and our churches, our institutions, and our nation. As they are growing up, the culture around them seeks to chip away at their beliefs, their ethics, and their hope. Still, the vast majority of all who receive Christ will do so by age eighteen. It is easy to see why we are passionate to reach them while they are most open to the gospel!

Identifying Your Passion

"Delight yourself in the Lord and He will give you the desires of your heart" (Psalm 37:4, NASB).

We are passionate about things that concern us, things we care deeply about. They may even burden us to the point of tears or grief. The problems facing young people today could leave us depressed if it wasn't for the avenue of prayer. As we present our hearts' concerns to God, He begins to turn our passion into vision – *His* vision – to meet the need that burdens us.

In the earliest days of our local networks, one of the priority activities was to form prayer fellowships. Keith Naylor was our national prayer coordinator. In a letter to the thirty-five prayer fellowship leaders in 1988 he said, "Prayer must be a priority — a time each week where people who have a heart for high school students fall before our Father on their knees and cry out to know and do God's will . . . When we pray, things begin to happen."

I believe that is the meaning of Psalm 37:4. Passion can come from many places, but when its source is God, we can trust it. The more we delight in the Lord and in His Word, the more His passions become the "desires of our hearts."

> The more we delight in the Lord and in His Word, the more His passions become the "desires of our hearts."

So what are the desires of your heart? Scripture tells us:

- "Love the Lord your God with all your heart . . . " (Mark 12:30)
- "Whatever you do, work at it with all your heart . . . " (Col 3:23)
- "Where your treasure is, there your heart will be also." (Matt 6:21)

Whatever is in your heart occupies your time, motivates your actions, and shapes your aspirations. Your heart is the rudder that directs your life.

Passionate Vision Takes Patience

Some of Oswald Chambers' much-loved, devotional thoughts came from talks he gave while ministering to troops at war in Egypt in the early 1900s. In an article called "Vision and Reality," Chambers gives insight about what is going on when God gives us a passionate vision and then seems to put on the brakes.

"We always have visions, before a thing is made real . . . God gives us the vision; then He takes us down to the valley to batter us into the shape of the vision. It is in the valley that so many of us faint and give way. Every vision will be made real if we will have patience . . . God has to take us through the fires and floods to batter us into shape, until we get to the place where He can trust us with the veritable reality . . . Don't lose heart in the process."[5]

Hang in there with the vision God has given you. Start by listening to the passion He has put in your heart. Then watch Him shape and mature the vision as you walk faithfully with Him.

"Better Together" Questions

Here are some questions that can help clarify your passion and vision. Some of the questions overlap, but I pray they will trigger helpful, personal insight.

1. What do you feel deeply burdened about and even moves you to tears? What burns within you that urges you to take action?

2. What has God put in your heart? What cause compels you and makes you want to give sacrificially or recruit others?

3. Why do you think God put you here on earth? How are you wired or gifted?

4. What brings you inner joy and fulfillment?

Chapter 2

HEART COMMITMENT

Surprisingly, the Network didn't start from a base of strong relationships – at least not at the first meetings. Many of us had never met. It was our shared passion to reach young people for Christ that motivated us. Our first gathering in 1979 had no formal agenda, no speakers, no intention of forming an organization or even holding another meeting. But it didn't take long for us to discover our common commitment – a desire to communicate the gospel to every teenager, to disciple those who respond, and to personally walk with Christ in every aspect of our lives.

Relationships are Built on Common Ground

That common commitment to teenagers formed a foundation for us to connect at the heart level. As we listened to each other, we could empathize and understand because we had similar passions. Yet the different perspectives stimulated interaction. Appreciation, respect, and open communication began to blossom. Our hearts were connecting.

Since that common commitment originated in God's heart, the relationships that flowed out of that passion were very special ones, empowered by the Holy Spirit who is identified in Ephesians 4:3 as the "Spirit of unity." Those relationships weren't just friendships. They were the beginning of a bond to follow God and His calling together. Two years later, we all signed a six-fold "Covenant" about our walk with Christ and our dedication to reaching teenagers for Him. Since then, we have continued to ask each member of the Network to review and recommit to the covenant annually.

When relationships are based in spiritual unity, it is not surprising that our connection with one another goes to a deeper level. Ephesians 4:16 illustrates this, using the example of a human body, which is united around Christ as the head: "From Him the whole body, joined and held together by every supporting ligament, grows and builds itself up in love, as each part does its work."

God Speaks Through Trusted Friends

God used the strong, heart commitment I had with several of my Network brothers to spare me from near disaster. Ministry burnout was looming for me, and I was blind to it. The Network was new, exciting, and gaining momentum. Membership growth was taking off, but person- nel and budget had not kept pace. I was so blessed to see the vision unfolding that I just kept plodding on. I did what I always did when the load got heavy – I got up earlier, stayed up later, and worked weekends. But the load never seemed to lighten.

The breaking point came at a board meeting when I presented four new proposals for the coming year – plans God had put on my heart. When the board vetoed two of the four ideas due to our limited capacity, I didn't see their wisdom or compassion. I just came away feeling discouraged and defeated.

Ecclesiastes 4:9-10 (NKJV) says: "Two are better than one . . . for if they fall, one will lift up his companion." That's what happened when two of my friends saved the day for me. Barry St. Clair and Billy Beacham were at the board meeting. They knew me well, and I trusted them to share truth with me. Their observations about seeing me "lose my joy" and "releasing the Network back to the Lord" were tough to hear. But because of our relationship, I knew they were trying to help me see what I couldn't – that I had let my own zeal and expectations pull me off course.

Those who were committed to me, including my wife and fellow staff member, Doug Tegner, helped me to set a *new* course. To this day, I am so thankful!

> I had let my own zeal and expectations pull me off course.

Come Alongside to Comfort

About a dozen youth workers met monthly in San Diego for breakfast – nothing too earth-shattering. Some in the area didn't feel they had time for all the chitchat with people they hardly knew, so they didn't come. But for those who did come, reservations and stereotypes were torn down, and relationships were built up over time.

Great ideas and resources were shared. Before long, so were confidences and personal concerns. Everyone was excited about the arrival of a new baby coming to one youth pastor's family. Tragically, a month after he was born, the baby died. Almost the entire Network was present for the funeral, seated in a solid row, right behind the family. Those youth workers – "coming alongside to comfort" (2 Corinthians 1:4) – were pillars of support and demonstrations of God's grace in our friend's journey to cope and heal.

We Need Each Other

One of our Network regional coordinators, Jason Kaat, explained to me how he discovered the value of networking:

> My calling to youth ministry was clear when I left college, but just three years later I was chewed up, confused, and ready to throw in the towel. My first church told me I wasn't good at programming and relating to adults so they fired me eight

months later. My second church didn't seem to be heading in the right direction   either. I wasn't seeing numerical growth. On the inside, I didn't feel I was "cool" enough to be a youth pastor.

Just when I was at the breaking point, I attended a retreat for youth workers. I got some time alone with Chris Renzelman, the Network's Northwest Regional Coordinator. I poured out my heart to him. He listened. I felt his genuine concern for me, for my soul. We didn't talk youth ministry strategy or how to appeal to students; we talked about my relationship with Christ.

In the months to follow, as we talked more, I saw that Chris was an example of how I wanted to minister to my students – modeling Christ's transforming grace to them, not worrying about the numbers. Repeatedly, in the years to come, I have built friendships with those in the Network who are committed to me, even when I've moved out of town – those who were not hesitant to ask me the hard questions, even about my family and personal life.

I did move on to a third church, but because I had a different perspective about ministry, I stayed for eight years. My longer tenure was a direct result of being a part of our network team. We were committed to become agents for change in our community. Today, I am honored to be a trusted leader in our school district as they see me pouring into the lives of middle school students. I am so thankful for my relationships in the Network that bore fruit in me – and now my relationships with others are multiplying that fruit.

Look for God's Guidance Through Relationships

Barry St. Clair was one of the primary architects of the Network. He was instrumental in the early organizational phase, helped write the Network

Objectives, Ministry Principles, and Covenant. He served as the chairman of the Network's Ministry Council for twenty years. He has been the embodiment to me of what this chapter is all about – deep, spiritual relationships that sharpen one another. But, my relationship with Barry pales in comparison to the story of another relationship. Let's let Barry tell it:

> In the early days of the Network, we gathered annually in the Colorado mountains for several days to enjoy each other (and the slopes), to talk about youth ministry, and to pray together about what we could do to make a difference. As we spent time praying for each other, confessing our sins – even crying together – we felt Jesus' presence. Deep friendships were formed.
>
> One of the deep friendships I formed was with Dave Busby. Dave was one of the most influential communicators to teenagers and youth leaders I have ever known. He became a regular speaker at our youth leader conferences. As I got to know him well, I learned that Dave was also the oldest, living cystic fibrosis patient in America. I prayed for him daily for eight years. In 1997 he went to be with Jesus.
>
> I had no idea what that loss felt like to Dave's wife Lawanna and her daughter. But, tragically, less than eight months later, I lost Carol, my wife of twenty-eight years. My kids and I experienced grief like we had never known.
>
> Just a few months later, at a Network Forum, a special service was held to honor Dave and Carol. Lawanna and I hardly knew each other, but we talked at the Forum about my close friend Dave. We emailed, and when we met again, our relationship started to blossom. Soon we were married! Little did I know the unpredictable way God would orchestrate His plan for our lives through our relationships in the Network!

Commit Hearts to What's Most Important

There are many levels of relationship that can be experienced in networking with others. It's exhilarating to discover those with similar interests, personalities, backgrounds, or even difficulties. It can be equally stimulating to connect with someone who is your polar opposite! And that is very possible since networking, by its very nature, draws diverse people together.

But networking, as described in these stories, is triggered when there is more "heart commitment" than just the novelty of a spontaneous connection. In those early Network meetings, the focus on reaching young people with the gospel stirred our hearts. As we prayed together, certain personal, rather than philosophical, themes began to emerge. We prayed about living holy lives, being godly models at home, discipling kids to follow Christ, sharing the gospel with every teenager, persevering in ministry, and being a resource to others.

> It can be equally stimulating to connect with someone who is your polar opposite!

By the time we met for the third year in 1981, we formulated a document that was a "covenant" with God and each other. It expressed our commitment to live by faith in the above aspects of our lives and ministries (see page 135). One by one we walked forward and signed our names. We all stood at the front and prayed together that God would empower us by His Holy Spirit and motivate us by our love for Christ and for young people to live out our faith in the six areas of the covenant that we signed.

> "A person standing alone can be attacked and defeated . . . two can stand back-to-back and conquer . . . three are even better . . ."

That "heart commitment" produced a powerful spiritual bond between us. The commitment continues and has spread to many others as fellow-workers across the country and around the world join us in the covenant. Over the years the covenant has been foundational, both in our relationships and in our journey to become more authentic Christ-followers. It has kept us moving in a united direction. Perhaps Ecclesiastes 4:12 (NLT) best explains this phenomenon: "A person standing alone can be attacked and defeated, but two can stand back-to-back and conquer. Three are even better, for a triple-braided cord is not easily broken."

"Better Together" Questions

1. Doug Fields, popular youth speaker and author, states that youth ministry is meant to be done in the context of relationships. Yet, he said, "I'm surprised at how unconnected some youth workers are." Is that you? Who shares your passion in ministry and interest in collaborating?

2. Who do you trust to tell you the truth about your life and ministry? How are you connecting with them?

3. Who do you know that would be encouraged if you "came alongside" to bless or help them?

4. Are there specific areas where you and your fellow workers help each other to stay committed to living out your faith? Is there any way to improve or move to the next level?

Chapter 3

SHARED PURPOSE

Two hundred fifty concerned parents, school counselors, sheriff's deputies, and local leaders jammed the community center in the small town of Poway, California. The community of 50,000   professionals and white-collar workers was not accustomed to much tragic news in their peaceful environs. Yet, in an eighteen month period, seven local teenagers had lost their lives in alcohol or drug-related incidents.

It was an emotional meeting as caring adults confronted the reality that sixty percent of kids at the largest area school might be using drugs, even heroin. A candid video of students speaking anonymously drove the point home. A brainstormed list of suggested action steps failed to promise any real solutions. Some left frustrated, even angry; most were just sincerely worried.

Daryl Nuss, the Network's Executive Director/CEO, was there. Standing in the back with others who packed the hall and looking over the crowd, Daryl did not see any other faith leader. He lamented that the church was missing a great opportunity to be present and to serve. As he traveled home, he couldn't shake the thought that it was up to him to make a move. "I don't have the time to get involved," he argued with himself. Still, he sensed the Lord asking him the question, "Will you make one phone call?"

The next morning, Daryl called the high school principal he knew and asked if they could meet to talk about how the faith community might come alongside the schools to address drug and alcohol abuse. The principal readily agreed to start the conversation. Four months later, over seventy-five Poway-area clergy, youth workers, law enforcement officials, and school leaders met to give their input about the issues and to discuss how they might work together for the good of the community. A steering committee was formed. More thoughtful conversation and initial steps of working together began to build a foundation of mutual trust between the faith community and school leaders.

The result? Five jointly-sponsored, interactive, parent workshops called, "What I Wish My Parents Knew," were held in three area schools. Almost 2,000 parents participated during the next three semesters, and the positive impact gave rise to continued efforts to work together to make a difference in their community.

An Urgent Goal

Sometimes it takes a critical situation to motivate people to come together to find solutions. That's what happened in Poway. The crisis of losing their kids to substance abuse became personal. These were their children. Children of parents just like them. Victims were friends of their children who were memorialized by flowers on street corners that they passed daily on their way to work.

The purpose of coming together became clear when it had faces attached to it – faces not only of the victims but also of their own children whom they were committed to protect and nurture. Suddenly, the need to take action was not someone else's responsibility. Like Daryl, those who had a clear vision of what needed to be done were compelled to step up to do their part. By becoming proactive, Daryl led the way to rally those who shared the vision to take ownership. They began to work together to start finding solutions. Did they solve the problem in three semesters? No, of course not. But they took positive steps. Doing nothing was not an option because of how much they cared for their kids.

That's really what brought the Network together. As described in the first two chapters, the shared purpose of reaching every teenager with the gospel gripped our hearts. But it wasn't until we came together and shared what each of us was doing that it really hit home how little

> Doing nothing was not an option because of how much they cared for their kids.

progress was being made. The more we focused on God's purpose for our ministries, the more we saw His heart in sending Jesus to "seek and save the lost" (Luke 19:10), "not wanting anyone to perish, but all to come to repentance" (2 Peter 3:9b). That clear and urgent purpose drove us to work together to accomplish it.

Assess the Needs and the Interest

While the Network was still in the formative stages, I was serving on the staff of Campus Crusade for Christ (now Cru). Following ten years of direct student ministry and working closely with local churches, Cru's high school national team asked me to lead a department that could serve youth workers nationwide. The initial idea was to sponsor the National Convention on High School Discipleship and to offer training for interested youth pastors on campus ministry.

I set out on a little "circuit riding tour" to get reactions and input from various ministry leaders. I'll never forget a meeting I had with the youth ministry leader of one church denomination. I came with my notepad, asking for suggestions on how church and parachurch ministries could work together to reach campuses more effectively. He shared candidly about the general perception of parachurch leadership. He felt that parachurch ministries tended to take students away from the church. It was a good, open discussion, but I still recall his resigned spirit as he concluded, "Frankly, I think it might be best if parachurch ministries just kept their focus on the campuses and left churches to take care of their own. It might not be right, but at least we wouldn't get in each other's way."

By contrast, in 1994 another church leader asked if he could present an idea to the Network's annual gathering of youth ministry executives and denominational leaders. He wanted their feedback on a new program they were planning to launch at the annual, national meeting. It was called "True Love Waits," a campaign for teenagers to make a public commitment to Christ about sexual purity. The response from the leaders was overwhelmingly positive, and most wanted to know how their groups could participate in the campaign. The leaders of the DC/LA national youth convention were so supportive that they offered to display all the commitment cards at the site of their closing rally on the Washington DC Mall. The result was an unforgettable expanse of 210,000 "True Love Waits" commitment cards, posted like a massive flower bed on the lawn of the nation's Capital.

What a dramatic reminder of the power of a shared purpose – one that, over the years, has shown dramatic results for purity in the lives of millions across the world.

Welcome Others of Like Purpose

Right after we were married, my wife and I served in our hometown of Portland, Oregon, with the high school ministry of Cru. We were seeing quite a bit of fruit; teenagers were responding and coming to Christ. It was pretty exciting. At the same time, I heard similar reports about a church ministry across town. I was curious and thought about getting together with this youth pastor, but I put it off. Finally, we arranged to have lunch. I didn't know why, but I was apprehensive about it.

First impressions didn't ease my insecurity. The youth pastor was very outgoing, athletic, and charismatic. As he shared his plan to reach kids and his vision for the whole city, I didn't feel excitement; I felt threatened! I was surprised at myself and ashamed that I had fallen so quickly into the trap of competitiveness. Both of us wanted to see our city reached for Christ. Both of us had a vision for ministry in every school, for staff to be raised up to disciple students, and for kids who would lead the way. Sort of sheepishly, I mustered, "Do you think there are some ways we could work together?" He responded resoundingly, "Of course!"

That was the beginning of a very rewarding partnership. At first, our networking was mainly through interaction and sharing ideas. Then I brought some staff and students to some of his events. Before long, our staff teams were interacting. We began to collaborate. Eventually, we co-sponsored a winter outreach retreat in the mountains. Two hundred students attended and a number of decisions for Christ were made. A wonderful side effect was that our kids got to observe their leaders working together. In time, other youth workers caught the vision, and the first local area network was growing its roots.

Finding Common Ground

By definition, networking draws people together from various backgrounds, doctrines, approaches, and methods. At first, when you don't know each other, there may be reluctance to open up – maybe even some misgivings or stereotypes about one another. This tendency is not uncommon or new.

In the seventeenth century it was religious conflict that set off the Thirty Years War, one of the longest and most destructive continuous wars in modern history. In 1627, Rupertus Meldenius, a German Lutheran theologian, was quoted in a tract appealing for Christian unity. This "early networking pioneer" gave us all a standard for how to seek the proper balance in working together for kingdom purposes:

In Essentials, Unity.
In Non-Essentials, Liberty.
In All Things, Charity.[6]

That is timeless wisdom, no doubt. But how do we get there? How do strong leaders with clear differences and dynamic visions establish common ground? What motivates them toward working together? Charles Finney, a leader in the Second Great Awakening in the early 1800s, said, "Nothing tends more to cement the hearts of Christians than praying together. Never do they love one another so well as when they witness the outpouring of each other's hearts in prayer."

> Nothing tends more to cement the hearts of Christians than praying together.

As basic and simplistic as that sounds, I believe it is a profound truth. I love helping to spawn a network by bringing together people who don't know each other but share a common purpose. It is often amazing how similar their prayers are. Some may have hesitancies or stereotypes to begin with, but hearing a sincere prayer from their brother or sister, even someone they do not know, often resonates with their own heart. God uses united prayer to build trusting bonds with those of like purpose.

In the body of Christ when we unite around our purpose, God "joins and knits us together . . . every part doing its share" to achieve His purpose in the big picture (Ephesians 4:16, NKJV). Now that's exciting!

"Better Together" Questions

1. Is there an urgent purpose you feel within that you just can't shake? What is the "one call" you could make to connect with someone else who might feel that same urgency?

2. Is there someone who might share your vision, someone with whom you are hesitant to connect? Isn't it worth a try to at least "break the ice"? How could you do that?

3. How could you broaden the circle of those who are committed to your purpose by praying with them? Who could you meet with in the near future?

Chapter 4

HUMBLE LEADERS

L et's leave our logos and egos at the door." Most of our Network forums and other network meetings include that challenge right up front. It's not meant as a rebuke – more as a reminder that crossing ministry lines requires some extra effort. Most of us are usually more comfortable in our own circles where we are known and loved. But at a network meeting, people may not know us, our accomplishments, or reputation. In that setting it's easy to begin comparing ourselves with others, referring to our successes, or even promoting the programs that excite us.

Not Caring Who Gets the Credit

My brother Warren and I used to joke about the book he planned to write: *Humility – and How I Attained It*. Humility is an elusive quality, isn't it? It's not something you can just set out to accomplish. "Lowliness of mind… esteeming others as better than himself" and "looking out for the interests of others" (Philippians 2: 3-4, NKJV) are not exactly natural to human nature.

One of my favorite quotes has always been: "There is no limit to what you can accomplish if you don't care who gets the credit."

Ironically, a tremendous number of people claim to have authored this classic statement! Still, it is very true. When we really care about a cause, we cheer for all who are contributing. Doing otherwise limits transparency and trust – and puts a big damper on collaboration.

Even when our motive, seeking to do God's will, is right, it is tempting to take what God shows us as our own personal mandate. My years with Cru acquainted me with its founder, Dr. Bill Bright, who signed every letter, "Yours for fulfilling the Great Commission in this generation." His visionary focus flowed through the entire organization. I know it made a great impact on me.

> There is no limit to what you can accomplish if you don't care who gets the credit.

Just prior to the meeting that gave rise to the Network in 1979, the national leaders of Cru's high school ministry met at their headquarters at Arrowhead Springs, California, to discuss a strategy to reach every teenager in the U.S. They shared their passion for the millions of lost teenagers and their burden to do more to reach them. As they knelt together to pray, the Spirit brought conviction to the whole group about how arrogant it was to assume that any one ministry could reach every teenager. Some wept, and there was a sense of God's lingering presence. When the group reconvened, the discussion shifted perspective from "How can *we* reach every teenager?" to "What *role* could we play in helping reach every teenager?" This proved to be a critical adjustment, paving the way for the idea to host a meeting of youth ministry leaders in 1979.

I've come to realize that God rarely gives a great idea to just one person. He usually plants it in a number of unique individuals and, in His mysterious way, weaves their efforts together to accomplish His purpose.

Transparency and Openness

2 Chronicles 7:14 is God's instruction to Israel that has become a guide which we seek to follow for revival in our day. I wonder if enough attention has been called to the first condition God names: "If my people

who are called by my name, will **humble** themselves. . . ." The pattern in Scripture is that God has never been impressed by those who are impressed with themselves, their possessions, or their accomplishments. Rather, He wants us to empty ourselves of those things so He can fill us fully with Himself. Talk about "contrary to human nature"! Everything within us wants to project success and shun failure. Yet, when we "humble ourselves before the Lord, He will lift you up" (James 4:10). Often this happens with the help of others.

At one Network Forum, Barry St. Clair spoke about personal holiness and invited those to come forward who wanted to confess moral sin and pray with someone about it. About fifty youth ministry leaders came to the front; many stayed late to pray and receive counsel. To me, this wasn't a sign of weakness but a sign of strength. They chose to depend upon God for help instead of themselves.

> I've come to realize that God rarely gives a great idea to just one person.

Atlanta 96, held in the Georgia Dome, was the largest-known meeting of youth workers ever held. It united leaders from every state and twenty countries. One of the mental pictures that stood out for many of us was seeing nearly 8,000 leaders on their faces, responding to Dave Busby's challenge to yield to God's call to intimacy. He prefaced that challenge by confessing his own struggles with his thought life. He then invited us to take off our shoes, making the place "holy ground" as we faced our own need for forgiveness and intimacy with God.

Transparency and openness with God and each other create an environment where God can accomplish His will. Sure, God can do whatever He wants whenever He wants, but He usually chooses to work through people. My favorite park is probably Yellowstone National Park. Beneath the surface, a large, flowing mass of hot, molten rock generates gases, steam, and heat which are the source of the hot springs and eruptions. In the same way that powerful pressure seeks release through a hole or porous spot, God is waiting to work through those who are open, yielded, and available.

"But we have this treasure in jars of clay to show that this all-surpassing power is from God and not from us" (2 Corinthians 4:7).

> In the same way that powerful pressure seeks release through a hole or porous spot, God is waiting to work through those who are open, yielded, and available.

Begin with Me

A student by the name of Evan Roberts was an unknown and unlikely instigator in the Welsh Revival of 1904-1905. He responded tearfully to an altar call with a simple yet heartfelt prayer, "Bend me, O Lord!" God answered Evan by transforming him and sending him throughout Wales with that message. He started by sharing his message with his youth group, and he saw sixty responses. He formed a traveling team to share the gospel and call believers to revival. At the end of a year, 100,000 converts were said to have been added to the Welsh Church. God "bent" Evan, and it impacted the church around the world.

Gypsy Smith was a well-known British evangelist in the nineteenth-century. A delegation once came to him to ask how they might experience personal and corporate revival as he had. Without hesitating, he said, "Go home. Lock yourself in your room. Kneel down in the middle of the floor, and with a piece of chalk, draw a circle round yourself. There, on your knees, pray fervently and brokenly that God would start a revival within that chalk circle. And don't leave that circle until God has answered your prayer."

We who live in the era of political, military, and technological power are still not accustomed to God's simple manner, shown in Scripture, where He accomplishes His will through humble means – aged parents, a shepherd boy, a widow's mite, loaves and fish, a baby in a manger.

But that is God's way. And although this is a book about networking, it really starts with one person walking humbly with God (Micah 6:8) and responding to His voice in obedience (1 Samuel 3). It is that individual's response that God may use to set in motion a whole network of people who will come alongside, but first, there is that one person who leads the way.

He accomplishes His will through humble means – aged parents, a shepherd boy, a widow's mite, loaves and fish, a baby in a manger.

At the very first See You at the Pole prayer event in Texas, Chuck Flowers shared a report he received from one of the 1,200 schools involved. This school had only one girl, standing alone, praying at her school's flagpole. When her youth pastor asked her afterward how she felt, she said, "I know that this morning I stood alone, but I know that there were thousands standing with me all across the state." That example prompted a wave of encouragement that is still felt today.

Earlier, I shared how the prayer meeting of Cru's national high school staff was instrumental in preparing the way for the first meeting that spawned the Network. But few people know that those first Network Forums might never have happened if Dan Maltby, one of those impacted by the meeting, had not stepped up to share his thoughts with the national director, Roger Randall.

After a moving prayer time, Dan felt a strong prompting to share with Roger his experience of networking with the YFC director when he was on staff in Washington DC. He described how fruitful it was for them to get together, share ideas, pray, and even co-host an event. He wasn't making any concrete suggestion, but he was just faithful to share what God had brought to his mind.

A few days later, Roger told Dan, "Let's hold a summit to bring a select group of youth ministry leaders together who care about reaching high school students." The result was the meeting held in January, 1979, and the rest is the Network's history. Who knows if that would have happened without Dan—one person responding to God's prompting.

"The Lord looks down from heaven on all mankind
to see if there are any who understand, any who seek God"
(Psalm 14:2).

"Better Together" Questions

1. What is the next setting you will be in where it would be wise to consider "leaving your logo and ego at the door"?

2. Think of a time it bothered you when you didn't get your rightful credit. Have you "let it go" yet?

3. How are you responding today to God's call to intimacy with Him? As with porous ground at Yellowstone Park, is your will yielded to Him so that He can easily find you open and available to display His power?

4. Has God brought revival to you? In what areas is He trying to "bend" you so you will be able to understand and follow Him more fully?

Chapter 5

MUTUAL TRUST

P eople are suspicious by nature – at least that's what I've seen in over thirty years of networking. The potential for unity is often threatened if others look, sound, act, or think differently than we do. Sometimes our hesitations to work together are from a healthy caution about diluting our energies or focus. But sometimes it's because we are so partial to our own ministry philosophy or approach that we quietly question if anyone else's is as valid as ours.

I remember hearing one person's response to criticism: "Well, maybe our way of doing it wrong is better than their way of not doing it!" Of course, they were jesting, but were they really?

> Sometimes ... we are so partial to our own ministry philosophy or approach that we quietly question if anyone else's is as valid as ours.

Fighting the Stereotypes

At early Network meetings when we talked about networking at the local level, I remember the skepticism that some people expressed. They thought it would be difficult to get certain denominations involved or some national youth ministries to be supportive. Some small churches were intimidated by the involvement of a big church in town. Others didn't have the time or see the need to network with anyone. Our sensitivities about ethnicity, gender, age, ministry philosophy, worship style, social issues (the list is endless), can work against our hopes of finding common ground to work together.

We faced this reality when we first considered the idea of hosting Atlanta 96, a joint event uniting a record number of youth workers from many denominations and youth organizations. I asked a group of leaders representing several groups, "What will it take for diverse ministries to get behind such an effort, to consider bringing their staffs, and even to do their annual training together?" I remember the immediate response from Lynn Ziegenfuss of Youth for Christ: "Mutual trust!" There was wholehearted agreement.

Partnership is a Process

If there is a "secret sauce" for the networking recipe, mutual trust is undoubtedly the main ingredient.

> If there is a "secret sauce" for the networking recipe, mutual trust is undoubtedly the main ingredient.

And although many youth workers today have developed a "taste" for networking, most of us still have plenty of room to grow in order to understand the process that true networking requires. The "Partnering Continuum" below is a great help in clarifying the process of partnering. It progresses from low to increasingly higher intensity in the areas of vision, relationships, sharing, commitment, structure, decision-making, interdependence, resources, risk, and control. Networking is multidimensional. In the spirit of Ecclesiastes 4:12, the Partnering Continuum is a cord of four strands: Connecting, Cooperating, Coordinating, and Collaborating. With the addition of each strand the "partnership cord" increases in strength.

Partnering Continuum

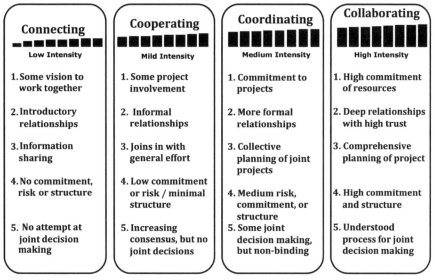

Connecting	Cooperating	Coordinating	Collaborating
Low Intensity	**Mild Intensity**	**Medium Intensity**	**High Intensity**
1. Some vision to work together	1. Some project involvement	1. Commitment to projects	1. High commitment of resources
2. Introductory relationships	2. Informal relationships	2. More formal relationships	2. Deep relationships with high trust
3. Information sharing	3. Joins in with general effort	3. Collective planning of joint projects	3. Comprehensive planning of project
4. No commitment, risk or structure	4. Low commitment or risk / minimal structure	4. Medium risk, commitment, or structure	4. High commitment and structure
5. No attempt at joint decision making	5. Increasing consensus, but no joint decisions	5. Some joint decision making, but non-binding	5. Understood process for joint decision making

© *REACT Services - 2014* / Info@REACTServices.com

Connecting

Connecting is where networking starts – meeting and interacting with others who share your common interest. However, it is only the first step. It amazes me that so many assume this is all there is to networking, and they are disappointed when this low-risk foray yields few outcomes. Still, it is a foundational "first strand" in weaving a strong cord for any partnership.

Before there was a network in the New York City area, I met there with about twenty area youth workers for lunch. Just before I was going to give a little talk, "casting the vision" for starting a network, I asked everyone to introduce themselves. That was as far as we got! The introductions alone served to open their eyes to much-needed resources right under their noses. They were so motivated that before they got halfway around the table they had already decided to meet every month!

At the 1995 Forum we invited leaders of fifteen aspects of youth ministry to connect in small "Dream Teams." One group included the

Youth Ministry Publishers, a group of common competitors who were rarely collaborators. They emerged from their meetings with smiles (thankfully), pleased with the opportunity to brainstorm with their colleagues about the felt needs of youth and youth ministry and how they could respond as publishers. They agreed, "It is time to build bridges and find ways to be more effective by working together."

Michael Hyatt, former CEO of Thomas Nelson Publishers, stated, "God didn't create a monochromatic world. He created a world with immense diversity . . . I want the best of everyone's thinking. It's an opportunity to create something much better when you have collaboration."[7]

> "...so we, who are many, are one body in Christ,
> and individually members one of another"
> (Romans 12:5, NASB).

Cooperating

After meeting and discovering each other's common interests, it is natural for leaders to discuss what they are doing in those common areas. A good example of the "Cooperating Level" is See You at the Pole, the national, student prayer event held on school campuses each September since 1990. Most of the basic elements are determined through the National Network of Youth Ministries – dates, theme, promotion, etc. Youth workers nationwide find it easy to be involved by promoting and participating. There doesn't have to be any formal commitment or big decision to make in order to be involved.

Cooperating is the kind of networking needed at most citywide and national events. They are already planned, promotion is prepared, and area leaders can simply decide to join in or not. When the Billy Graham Crusade came to San Diego in 2003, they asked the local network to promote their Youth Night. Advance notice was unusually short, but because the network had seventeen local chapters in the county, word traveled fast.

An estimated 74,000 youth attended, one of their largest youth events, with hundreds receiving Christ as Savior.

> "…be like-minded toward one another…that you may with one mind and one mouth glorify the God and Father of our Lord Jesus Christ" (Romans 15:5-6, NKJV).

Coordinating

To bring 8,000 youth leaders together for Atlanta 96 illustrated the Partnership Continuum in several respects, but for many it was a "Cooperation Level" activity. Most people remember Atlanta 96 for the musicians, speakers, and exhibits in the Georgia Dome and for the 10,000 students who joined in with their "True Love Waits" commitment cards stacked to the roof, twenty-seven stories high, but that was only part of the event.

"Every Kid, Every Campus, Every Community" for Christ.

The other half of the event demonstrated the Coordinating Level. Thirty-six diverse ministries sponsored mini-conferences at venues close to the Georgia Dome. These ministries not only cooperated, but also made specific commitments to *coordinate* their efforts, become more formally structured, and take on more risk (e.g. hotel contracts) and responsibility (e.g. program).

The overall impact of this increased commitment brought unprecedented unity among ministries and launched a national campaign to reach "Every Kid, Every Campus, Every Community" for Christ.

Collaborating

The outgrowth of this campaign to reach every student, school, and community for Christ was called "Challenge 2000." Its goal was to establish a ministry to every junior high and high school by the year 2000. We realized that this would take far more than "cooperating" or even "coordinating" around a catchy, conference slogan. It would take higher commitment, deeper relationships, more structure, joint decision-making, and greater risk of resources and reputation. In short, it would require the highest level of "mutual trust," earmarked "collaboration" on the Partnering Continuum.

Leaders of the Atlanta 96 sponsoring organizations and national campus ministries met to confirm their commitment, direction, and plan to accomplish the goals of "Challenge 2000." The members of this new steering committee represented the diversity of doctrine and ministry approach. Their joint commitment to unity was a wonderful testimony to the work of the Spirit. The original intent was to disband the campaign in 2000. But after five years of relationships and co-laboring, the drive to complete the task was strong. They chose to continue working together under the name Campus Alliance. Today, the group has developed into its own ministry with the Network as a partner in the continuing effort to reach every middle school and high school student.

The Process Illustrated

By definition, the parts of a continuum are not meant to operate separately but rather as an integrated progression from one element to another. Granted, nothing in ministry seems that orderly, but it is certainly the hope of all of us who are committed to networking that no one remains only at the "Connecting" level, but rather experiences the greater fruit of the steps toward "Collaborating." As in the body of Christ, each part is meant to coordinate with the whole. "From him the whole body, joined and held together by every supporting ligament, grows and builds itself up in love, as each part does its work" (Ephesians 4:16).

> The parts of a continuum are not meant to operate separately but rather as an integrated progression from one element to another.

The integration of the four levels is not usually "seamless." The urban network spent years at the "Connecting" level. Urban ministries in each city had unique needs for networking, and we wondered if we would ever launch a *national,* urban initiative. At the Network forums in Colorado, urban "cooperating" began simply – with commitments to stay in touch and pray for each other. Urban networking advanced to the "coordinating" level when key individuals were willing to step up to lead. For example, Margaret Struder, Fred Lynch, and Chris Brooks each took a turn, like relay runners, in advancing the cause a little further.

Then in January, 2006, a National Urban Networks Summit was held in Orlando that set the stage for the "collaborating" level. Passionate and diverse urban leaders from across the country gathered to share resources, expertise, and best practices. This group identified key needs of urban youth workers and set in motion a strategic plan, advisory board, urban database, resource list, and website. They helped fund a coordinator and launched a two-day prayer summit to intercede for the launch of their efforts.

It took over ten years for the urban network to move through the "Partnering Continuum," but it was worth it to see urban youth workers connect and share resources and training that otherwise may not have been available.

Building Bridges When There is a Trust Gap

If unity was so important to Jesus (John 17:21), then disunity must be a priority in Satan's strategy. Often we play into Satan's hand by letting difficulties, differences, stereotypes, or resistance cause a breach of trust. Here are some examples of how bridges can be built.

Differences of doctrine and approach. Initially, some denominations and organizations were hesitant about networking due to differing doctrines and ministry philosophies. But we've found that unity stands a better chance when we focus on our commonalities (e.g., purpose and principles) rather than on our differences. Billy Beacham (Student Discipleship

Ministries) shares his perspective: "I have many lifelong friends through the Network that I grew to love before I knew their theological beliefs. Even now that I know some of their beliefs are considerably different than mine, our relational bond is still greater than our differences."[8] ***The Bridge: Relationships***.

No compelling desire to network. I met with two national urban leaders who were negative about networking; they couldn't envision it being effective in their circles. In another instance, a megachurch youth pastor friend told me he didn't need to network and didn't have the time to be involved with others who did feel the need. In both those instances, God gave me patience to listen and not judge. Sure, I offered my views, but I realized that pressuring them would work against building trust. Until they had an internal desire, we would have to wait on God's timing – both for them to see the need and for us to find other leaders. We had to wait several years, but God answered. UrbNet was raised up (as described above) and served their ministries. The youth pastor moved to plant a church. Suddenly he saw the need to partner, and he is now one of the Network's strongest advocates. ***The Bridge: Patience***.

People seeking only their own interests. Some view a network as a golden opportunity to promote their ministry, product, or service. That's okay. One of the functions of a network is to share resources, but when it appears this is the only reason they are involved, it can destroy trust. "Do not merely look out for your own personal interests, but also for the interests of others" (Philippians 2:4, NASB). In a Network event that involved a number of speakers on the program, clear time and topic limitations were in place. If speakers disregarded those standards, especially if they had something to promote, they lost credibility with the audience, and, in some cases, people lost trust in them and their ministry. Everyone makes mistakes, especially when you are passionate about your vision, so a network needs to be patient in the spirit of Ephesians 4:2-3:

" . . . bearing with one another in love, endeavoring to keep the unity of the Spirit in the bond of peace." *__The Bridge: Grace__*.

Disconnectedness within the Network. Maybe the group is just starting or maybe there's a lack of chemistry. Rural youth ministry leaders from eight areas of the country gathered for the first time. Though each was extremely effective in their home area, they didn't know each other. They introduced themselves, their ministries, and the needs they saw. It was apparent that most came to the meeting feeling they were a solitary voice advocating for rural youth ministry. But that feeling vanished when they started praying. Each one, praying about his or her vision, fanned the flame of vision in the others.

You could sense their connectedness growing as they heard others share visions for rural ministry similar to their own. The trust that grew out of that meeting formed the foundation of what was soon to become a national coalition of rural ministries. *__The Bridge: Praying Together__*.

Mutual Trust Starts with Trusting God

The Great Commission to go with the gospel to the entire world (Matthew 28:18-20) was a command Jesus gave to *all* his disciples to accomplish in unity. In John 17:21, when Jesus spoke of the world believing in Him, the priority in His prayer was that believers would be one with each other and with Christ and His Father. That gives a new meaning to "mutual trust." We trust each other because we trust God and His plan to redeem the world through oneness. What an awesome thought that God wants to accomplish such a significant task through you and me, working together – and with Him!

> We trust each other because we trust God and His plan to redeem the world through oneness.

Once we trust the truth of what God wants to accomplish through oneness, we can roll up our sleeves to begin working together. Galatians

6:2 (NKJV) says to, "Bear one another's burdens . . . " This assumes that we will help the others who have a need and that we will trust them enough to allow them to help us with *our* needs. This will "fulfill the law of Christ" which I understand to be the law of love – loving God, your neighbor and yourself (Matthew 22:37-40).

Mutual trust is at the heart of networking. It leads us to unity because it is an expression of our love for God and our love for each other.

"Better Together" Questions

1. Are you hesitant to work with those who do ministry differently than you? What does it take to develop trusting, working relationships with someone?

2. Can you think of an instance where networking with a person outside of your ministry stimulated a fresh thought or action? What led you to trust that input?

3. People tend to rush to the Collaborating Level before they have developed strong relationships and have adequately assessed the amount of commitment and risk involved. Why do you think that is? What needs to be done for you to avoid that mistake?

4. If we accept that God plans to use our oneness with others as a primary tool to reach the world, what more could we do to better align ourselves with that plan?

Chapter 6

BIG DREAMS

Expect great things from God. Attempt great things for God."
It was more than a catchy phrase. It was the outline of an historic sermon by William Carey in 1792,[9] intended to move fellow pastors to join him in taking the Great Commission seriously and personally. His text was Isaiah 54:2-3, "Enlarge the place of your tent" – to the nations, to the "desolate cities." But the initial response from the pastors was not positive. At a follow-up meeting, they said the missionary challenge was too big. Carey's impassioned appeal to his close friend Andrew Fuller seemed to help change the tone of the meeting.

A cooperative effort established the first missionary society.

Carey's persistent attempt to do "great things for God" resulted in a cooperative effort that established the first missionary society and helped recruit missionaries to go with him to India to ultimately communicate the gospel and translate the Bible into Bengali, Sanskrit, and other languages. Together they raised funds, organized the means for missionaries to live in community, and patiently ministered in India for seven years before God gave them their first Hindu convert. Carey is widely regarded as the "father of modern missions."[10]

Hear God's Calling

God is the one who determines if what we attempt for Him is "great." It is His "Well done, good and faithful servant" that we seek (Matthew 25:23). But we can be sure of one thing that *is* great – His calling on our lives. While God calls each of us to unique areas of service, His call is to <u>all of us</u> in several areas – for instance:

1. A Godly Life

Reaching "every" is such a "big dream" for me, I almost made it the chapter title. But that's only part of God's calling. For those with "passionate visions" (Chapter 1), it is easy for the "cause" to be so all-consuming that we march on without our Leader. I've worked with some who were outstanding leaders, yet their hearts for God were secretly being sabotaged. It can happen to anyone, no matter how well-meaning.

It can happen to you.

It can happen to me.

Jesus posed a question that would be so heartbreaking to ever hear from Him: "Why do you call me, 'Lord, Lord,' and do not do what I say?" (Luke 6:46). Obedience is at the heart of godliness and foundational to making it through the storms of life (Luke 6:47-49), but it can be very hard to stand alone. We get blindsided by a wave we didn't see or a trend we ignored. We need that reliable partner or trusted team to lift us up (Ecclesiastes 4:9-12).

The first thing the leaders did, after agreeing to form the National Network of Youth Ministries in 1981, was to sign a written covenant with God and with each other in six areas of life and ministry (see page 136). It was a high standard (Ephesians 4:1), but there was strength in knowing that others were walking with us. As the Network grew, thousands more joined in that commitment. I still have my original covenant although it is yellow and worn. It's a reminder of God's calling and of those who are my partners.

2. The Great Commission

Jesus gave everyone the calling to take the message of reconciliation to the world (2 Corinthians 5:18-20) and to make disciples (Matthew 28:18-20). There is something so compelling to me about the fact that God "wants *all people* to be saved and to come to a knowledge of the truth" (2 Timothy 2:4). That is every person, everywhere (Mark 16:15).

> Everyone has a right to know the truth about Jesus Christ – every class, every color, every ethnic group, every segment of our society.

At the Atlanta 96 Youth Leaders Conference, I had the challenging job of leading the planning for the joint sessions of this largest-ever, youth worker gathering. We asked, "What would Jesus say to His youth ministers if He had them all in one place?" Among other very personal things, we felt Jesus would want us to invest ourselves completely in reaching the fifty percent of the population who are under eighteen and most open to the gospel. Consequently, our theme was "every" – "Every Kid, Every Campus, Every Community." Youth workers signed the "Challenge 2000 Covenant" (see page 136) and were encouraged to take it home for their youth groups to sign. The covenant targeted what could be accomplished by the year 2000.

It is critically important to keep God's big-picture perspective before us and not to "lose sight of the forest for the trees." Our tendency is to become absorbed with all that's going on in our "grove of trees." Jim Rayburn, founder of Young Life's phenomenal ministry to teenagers, gave this final message titled, "Stay Committed to the 'Big Dream'," to the Young Life staff before he died:

> Everyone has a right to know the truth about Jesus Christ – every class, every color, every ethnic group, every segment of our society.
> Everyone needs Jesus Christ.

They have a right to know who He is. They have a right
to know what He's done for them. They have a right to know
Him personally. They have a right to make their own choice
of Him.

If there's ever a generation in human history that needed
to hear that, it's now! . . . There's no price too high to pay to
see to it that young people have a chance to know the Savior.[11]

3. Love and Serve One Another

Jesus said our greatest calling is to love God first and then our neigh-
bors (Matthew 22:38-39). Networking, in my experience, is a response to
Jesus' command, "Love each other as I have loved you. Greater love has
no one than this: that he lay down his life for his friends" (John 15:12-
13).

In Columbus, Indiana, a teenage girl acted on her love for those in
Uganda who were without safe water and sanitation. With the help of the
Columbus Area Youth Ministries Alliance, five churches came behind her
to help raise the $40,000 needed for an international ministry to
provide sustainable water for one community. They didn't just meet their
goal. They surpassed it! It was satisfying to know that her networking
enabled her to "love each other . . . using whatever gift you have received
to serve others" (1 Peter 4:8-10).

God's call to love was always a radical challenge. In the early   seventeenth century, a series of wars in Europe wreaked havoc for three
decades. Religious disputes between Anglicans, Presbyterians, Congrega-
tionalists, and other denominations compelled peacemakers like British
pastor, Richard Baxter, to urge fellow clergy to set the example of love
and unity. His letter written in 1656 still applies today:

It is required for us to be united as fellow laborers . . . As
ministers we should lead in the initiatives that prevent divisions
and that seek healing . . . Instead of quarreling with our brethren,
let us rather cooperate against our real and common adversaries.

That is why it is important for ministers to associate and to enjoy friendships . . . We must do the work of the Lord in unity and harmony . . . to avoid misunderstandings and to consult for mutual edification. To maintain love and communion together is what the word of God has commanded us to do.[12]

God's calling is the source of the "big dreams" He has for our lives in the three areas mentioned above. But think how our abilities to fulfill those dreams are "better" when we are "together"—not only with each other but with God Himself. For instance:

1) Living a godly life comes from an intimate and abiding relationship with Him. When we network, we can "encourage one another daily" (Hebrews 3:13) to keep that relationship fresh.

2) The Great Commission is an enormous challenge to multiply disciples, but when Jesus gave it to us, He also gave us "all authority" (Matt 28:18)!

3) Loving and serving others flows out of our experience of His great love for us (1 John 4:19). Networking enhances this experience through the many resources that become obvious as we connect.

God's calling on our lives transforms our reason for living. If we yield to the "big dreams" He has for us, we can, through the power of His Spirit, be sure of making an impact for His kingdom. And, one day, we will be hearing God's glorious affirmation, "Well done!"

Find your Niche

In Galatians 1:1-2 the apostle Paul was called to ministry, but he was prepared from birth for his specific calling—to preach the gospel to the Gentiles (Galatians 1:15-16). Likewise, God has a unique role for each of us to play in His eternal plan.

At one of the Network's gatherings of national, youth ministry executives, the representative of the Assemblies of God/Youth Alive, Jay Mooney, told me about trying to find his role at the table as the leaders discussed working together in campus ministry. A Fellowship of Christian Athletes (FCA) leader mentioned that they might consider changing their campus ministry name to "Fellowship of Christian Students." FCA Vice President, Kevin Harlan, differed with his fellow-staffer. "It's not who we are," Kevin said. "Our ministry is to athletes." That made the light go on for Jay. Jay shared it this way with me:

"It was so helpful for me to see that the expectation in a network is not that we have to be everything to everyone. Our uniqueness is valuable to the group. We need to be who we are to the best of our ability. It helped me know how I could work with the whole diverse group, giving freely while not feeling like I'm abandoning my commitment to my own ministry."

A good Network respects diversity of gifts and callings. By so doing, it also surfaces opportunities for those with the same niche to find common ground. When the conversation turns to rural or urban or campus ministries, people of like mind are almost magnetically drawn together! In youth ministry, we have identified "Affinity Networks" which encourage a coordinator and leadership team to facilitate the leveraging of strategies and resources.

One Affinity Network focused on campus outreach. Reaching kids at school has been a part of the Network's DNA since its first set of objectives in 1981. And when the Supreme Court upheld the Equal Access Act in 1990, the Network was in the right place at the right time to fan the flame of thousands of student-led, campus, Christian clubs. We invited campus ministry leaders to strategize nationally, starting with a Campus Ministry Summit in 1993 and "Dream Teams" at the Network forum in 1995. At the Atlanta 96 Youth Leaders Conference the entire audience of 8,000 split up by states and communities. They examined lists of nearby schools that had no campus ministries and discussed what to do.

At Atlanta 96 "Challenge 2000" was announced. It set our sights on the goal of establishing a ministry to every secondary school in America. We recognized that, without a united effort and the power of the Spirit, it would be nothing more than a "big dream." However, thousands of delegates and sixty-two national ministries agreed to cooperate! These groups represented 100,000 churches, 250,000 youth workers, and 2.5 million Christian students. The Maclellan Foundation came behind the effort with their largest grant ever given to youth ministry. By the year 2000, research and records revealed that the number of "Challenge 2000"-related school ministries had grown from 12,000 to 35,000 in the 56,000 schools, almost a two-hundred percent increase in five years.[13] The growth was remarkable, but the campus ministry leaders could not leave unfinished the task of establishing ministries at the remaining schools. This partnership of ministries continues today. It is known as the Campus Alliance.[14]

Believe God – and Expect Challenges

The reason that we can "attempt great things for God" is that we believe in the validity of God's calling on our lives. We believe that He will equip us to fulfill that call (1 Corinthians 12:7) and that He will produce fruit as we work in cooperation with others (1 Corinthians 3:6). By faith we "expect great things *from* God."

Jesus said this differently in John 14:12, but to me it is one of the most mind-boggling verses in the entire Bible. " . . . Whoever believes in Me will do the works I have been doing, and they will do even greater works than these. . . . " A few verses later He explains that this is because He is sending the Holy Spirit. Jesus is not implying that we will *be* greater than Him – of course not! He's just saying that His plan for reaching the world means we will *do* greater works than He did. He had "big dreams" for the disciples He was speaking to, but they weren't pipedreams. He was providing the Holy Spirit to bring these dreams to reality, enabling the disciples to, for example, travel more widely and see more conversions than He ever did. It's still mind-boggling, isn't it?

As exciting as it is to realize that God's big dreams for us can be fulfilled in the Spirit, you can be sure that there will be nightmares to go along with some of them. When we started the Network, Dr. Howard Hendricks of Dallas Seminary heard our ideas and said, with his typical fervor, "What you are suggesting has never been done. You may have to go through hell and high water to do it, but it will be worth it!"

I confess. In sharing the stories of past cooperation I focused on the positive results. Yes, at Youth Congress 85, thousands of teenagers were trained when two large organizations miraculously decided to cooperate. But I didn't tell you about the two electrical fires at the Washington Hilton Hotel that ousted almost 4,000 of our delegates for two nights in a row, closing down that famous hotel for six weeks.

I told you about powerful moments at Atlanta 96 with youth workers praying and celebrating in the Georgia Dome. But I didn't tell you about the chaos and near disruption in one of the general sessions when House Security, armed with bullhorns and handguns, tried to protect someone who had received a threat.

We are impressed by William Carey's diligence as the "father of modern missions." But you may not know that his wife had a complete nervous breakdown and that three missionaries on his small team died of illnesses, including his own son.

> Big dreams come with big challenges, even when we are acting upon God's calling.

Sorry to end the chapter with this dose of reality, but it's good to remember that big dreams come with big challenges, even when we are acting upon God's calling and in the power of His Spirit. This generation expects positive outcomes from their work, and they expect those positive outcomes very quickly! But God's timetable is not limited to our lifetimes. In Hebrews 11, those in the "Hall of Faith," like Noah and Abraham, "did not receive the things promised" before they died (11:13).

Look again at John 14:12. Jesus said that His promise of doing "greater works" is reserved for those who "believe in Me." That's the path we must take if we want to fulfill God's calling and "big dreams" in our lives.

"Better Together" Questions

1. In the category of "greater works" that Jesus said we could do in the power of the Spirit, what are your biggest needs? Take a moment to submit them to God, believing Him for supernatural results!

2. In terms of what you are focused on today, what is God's "big picture"? (How do your "trees" fit into His "forest"?)

3. Is there any way you are more attached to your "big dream" than you are to the Author of that dream?

4. What is your unique role in the cause to which you are committed? How can you maximize that?

Chapter 7

LEVERAGED RESOURCES

Working together just makes sense. In physics it is called "leveraging." Leveraging overcomes obstacles by strategically focusing resources that dramatically increase our ability to move forward. Every lever has a "fulcrum" (or pivot point) that is central to the lever's capacity. That's where a network fits into the analogy; it's the pivot point that unites diverse individuals and resources for accomplishing together what could not be accomplished alone.

Networking is all about "Two are better than one because they have a good return for their work" (Ecclesiastes 4:9). But when it says that "a cord of three strands is not quickly broken," think of the leveraging power when that third strand is God!

> "A cord of three strands is not quickly broken." Think of the leveraging power when that third strand is God!

Put your Network in Place

Every year the Network holds a meeting for the top leaders of youth ministry organizations. It was our privilege to be hosted for a briefing at the White House in 2003. Bob Flores, Director of the Department of Juvenile Justice, came to greet us. As he surveyed the group of thirty-four national youth ministry leaders, he asked me privately, "Are these groups mentoring kids?"

"Well," I said, "if your definition includes 'discipling,' I would say, 'Yes, most definitely!'"

Mr. Flores responded, "Currently, there are over 500,000 young people on waiting lists for an adult mentor. The president is trying to recruit a million more. Do you think you could help us?"

That conversation set in motion four months of rigorous dialogue which led to four years of federal grants to fund a nationwide mentor recruitment strategy from the faith community. This unprecedented opportunity presented itself because federal officials saw the potential of what the Network could accomplish through leveraging. Those thirty-four ministries represented thousands of youth workers and hundreds of thousands of adults. But the officials needed our network of trust and relationships to locate new resources to help meet the need.

Our first task was to prepare our networks by planning how to communicate the vision and opportunity to our own local networks and national partners. In order for the strategy to work, they would be the key players in recruiting and equipping what we called "Mentor Recruitment Ambassadors" from their churches and organizations. Though the program wasn't a fit for everyone, those who did participate worked with us to create a website, printed and online promotion, twenty-five new mentoring resources, and other means that mobilized thousands of mentors and hundreds of new mentoring programs.

In fact, our leveraged efforts actually multiplied themselves. Because we were using new methods to recruit more mentors from the churches, the greater mentoring community (beyond the faith-based groups) asked us to host national, training conferences to share our resources and strategies in four locations. So by working together, God enabled us to make a contribution to meet an urgent need, but He leveraged it far beyond what we could ever have imagined!

Gather People and Resources

The tragic shootings at Columbine High School in 1999 took fifteen lives and injured many more. In the months to follow, other traumatic events nationwide served as wake-up calls for communities to be better prepared. Many of these communities have local networks of youth workers. These leaders from churches and local youth organizations are usually among the first responders on the scene of a crisis to provide counseling, reach out to families, and help students process what has just happened. However, most of these leaders have never been officially trained or certified. Thus, they are not recognized by the school and community officials as part of the intervention team, like the Red Cross and other emergency professionals. This was epitomized at Columbine because it took considerable time for the federal grief counselors and other agencies to arrive. Youth workers had been on the scene from the outset, but they had limited access.

Network leaders realized that they needed to step up to help maximize the number of youth workers and caring adults who would be resources for a crisis when it hits their communities. Because of the relationships youth workers already had with the students and their families, it was natural for them to help in the healing and recovery process.

The Network developed what we called "Critical Incident Response Teams" to offer four levels of training for youth workers in communities everywhere. Materials and seminars generated higher levels of preparedness. In cooperation with national credentialing agencies, the training facilitated relationship-building and greater credibility for faith-based youth workers, enabling them to serve as co-equals alongside other emergency personnel. This resulted in more opportunities to serve the needs, including the spiritual needs, of teenagers and families in crisis.

Launch a United Effort

In the battle for the hearts and minds of today's youth there may be times when we feel like we are "charging hell with a squirt gun." And while it's true that we can't win in this spiritual battle without God's power and protection, He usually enacts His will through the cooperative efforts of His children.

> While it's true that we can't win in this spiritual battle without God's power and protection, He usually enacts His will through the cooperative efforts of His children.

When Nehemiah was led to rebuild the wall of Jerusalem, he got the king's permission, put his plan in place, and made preparations. But then came the time for action. "Let us rise up and build" (Nehemiah 2:17-18). Surely, it was a daunting task. Even the officials laughed at them. But they took the initiative with confidence, knowing that God delights in displaying His power though His people as they work together.

Picture ninety-five streams and rivers converging one by one from northern Minnesota to the Gulf of Mexico. For 2,340 meandering miles, water converges from thirty-one states and two Canadian provinces. What started as a trickle in some places eventually becomes the Mighty Mississippi, North America's largest river delta.

So take heart from God's pattern of gladly accepting our "little" and making it "much." Even the magnitude of the Mighty Mississippi can't compare to the power of our Mighty God!

In 1983, Youth for Christ and Campus Crusade for Christ were planning to hold separate national youth conferences in 1985. The Network had just started, but this "young buck" (me) felt prompted to appeal to the leaders of these two national organizations to consider working together in order to leverage their resources and accomplish even more than they could alone. It was just a simple lunch meeting, but God used it as a catalyst for an unprecedented collaboration called Youth Congress 85. The 16,000 teenage delegates came to the Washington DC Convention Center from 7,000 high schools, every state, and thirteen countries. They received outreach training from experienced campus staff members and were inspired in general sessions by leaders like Chuck Colson, Bill Bright, Jay Kesler, and Josh McDowell.

They left DC believing the theme, "We can make a difference now and forever." And many of them did make a difference – like Sherri McCready who returned home to Wichita, Kansas, and started a campus Bible study group at her high school. By the end of that year there were student-led Bible study groups at eight area high schools, spreading eventually to every high school in Wichita and continuing to this day.

Three years later, the desire persisted to leverage resources for training youth nationally. Youth Congress 85 was followed-up by the triennial DC/LA conventions which continued on both coasts for over twenty years, training over 150,000 teenagers.

Putting It All Together

Sometimes it may seem simpler to "go it alone," but there is so much evidence that we are *better together.*

Over the years, so many youth workers with similar "callings" and expertise have discovered each other. Unified by their passionate focus to reach a specific segment of the culture, they chose to leverage their efforts rather than stay to themselves. "Affinity Networks" began forming to pray together, build relationships, and share strategies and resources. One of the things I love most about networking is to see those of common passion connect with one other: ministries to campus, urban, rural, Native Americans, missions, deaf teens, Women in Youth Ministry, critical incident response, mentoring, and the Youth Transition Network. They followed the steps above to: 1) put a network in place, 2) gather people and resources, and 3) initiate a united launch.

> Sometimes it may seem simpler to "go it alone," but there is so much evidence that we are *better together.*

Michael Hyatt of Thomas Nelson Publishers admitted:

> For years I was a solo practitioner. I didn't really invite people into my life to work with me. I thought I didn't really need anybody else until I took some hard tumbles myself. Then I realized, "No, I desperately need people." It's a lot more fun when I collaborate. When we work alone, we get really used to having it our way and doing what we want when we want to do it. We don't have to listen to or answer to anybody else. People are going to have different perspectives from you. They're not wrong; they're just seeing stuff you don't see. What I like about collaboration is that it forces me to grow . . . Sure, it's a lot slower than being a dictator. But if I'm secure, I'm comfortable with inviting outside input . . . it's more effective over the long haul.[15]

Sometimes one partner carries more of the load than another. Billy Beacham, president of Student Discipleship Ministries and a major partner in supporting See You at the Pole, said, "We are so much stronger and more effective together. However, this often means a lot of work. We just helped sponsor a Network function and ended up carrying most of the load. You have to firmly hold to a kingdom mindset . . . keeping your focus on the greater cause."[16]

There is an Ethiopian proverb, *"When spider webs unite, they can tie up a lion."* That isn't just a metaphor. Though I couldn't find a picture of a lion caught in a spider web, scientists say it is actually possible! Pound for pound, a spider's silk is many times stronger than steel. The only problem is getting enough spiders to leverage their resources – the same problem we have with many of the challenges we face.

"Better Together" Questions

1. In the example of spider webs tying up a lion, the limitation is not the quality of the spider's silk but the quantity that is required. In your network, you probably have many gifted people. What is the "critical mass" you need to tackle your issue of greatest concern? How can you expand the number of those committed to solve it?

2. How is your network doing as the "pivot point" for leveraging diverse resources to accomplish something greater than could be done alone? What is your current focus?

3. Who are the people and what are the resources you need in order to leverage the maximum impact on the issues you are concerned about?

4. Is there something that you are feeling prompted to do (big or small) to help launch the dream that you and others are seeking to accomplish?

Chapter 8

UNITED PRAYER

The story is told of a very wealthy man who threw a lavish party at his mansion. He spared no expense for his friends, including adorning his large swimming pool with a great white shark! Impulsively, he announced, "I will give anything I own to the person who swims across that pool."

When no one responded, the party continued until suddenly there was a big splash, and everyone ran to the pool. They discovered a man swimming frantically with the shark chasing, and jaws snapping. Just as the shark was about to overtake him, he reached the other side, escaping death by the thinnest of margins. The wealthy man shook his hand and said, "You are the bravest person I have ever met. Of all I have, what can I give you?" Breathless, the man said, "For starters, how about giving me the name of the guy who pushed me in?"

How did you come to realize the importance of prayer? If you are like me, the conviction didn't come automatically. Most of us, like the swimmer in the shark-infested pool, don't think much about prayer until we are in over our heads – until the only way to survive our circumstances is to plead for God to rescue us. Even then, most people tend to rely on their own strength instead of turning to God. Amazing! So many sharks, so little prayer!

Our Neck or God's Will?

God invites us to be partners in accomplishing His will on earth. When the Holy Spirit indwells and empowers us, it brings us into union with God in accordance with Jesus' prayer (John 17:21). Prayer is bringing my will into alignment with God's will (Matthew 6:9-10). It means attuning my desires to His desires (Psalm 37:4-5) and yielding my circumstances to His overall design (Psalm 57:2). So then, prayer is not so much about us and our urgent needs as it is about submitting to God and His will.

> Prayer is not so much about us and our urgent needs as it is about submitting to God and His will.

The good news is that when we are praying according to His will "in whatever we ask, we know that we have the requests which we have asked from Him" (1 John 5: 14-15).

While this experience with God is very personal, we often found that the experience of seeking God's will is intensified when we pray with others. About ninety percent of all Scripture on prayer has to do with corporate prayer, according to David Bryant, respected prayer ministry leader and author. He says, "Praying together increases awareness of and heart commitment to the purposes and mission of Christ, the way little else can." [17]

Uniting our prayers with other believers is what is called for in the revival passage of 2 Chronicles 7:14. The apostle Paul also spoke of it as a key to helping his ministry team rely on God and endure difficulties "in answer to the prayers of many" (2 Corinthians 1:10-11).

Praying with Partners

United prayer may start small. Sometimes there are personal issues or private concerns that we are not meant to bear alone but are best kept to a small circle of trusted friends (Galatians 6:2). The Network has been a safe place to connect in that way – at local networks, at conferences, or even with student "Prayer Triplets." Groups of two or three can gather quickly to support each other "if one falls down" (Ecclesiastes 4:10), or act as a "cell group" to meet for prayer on a regular basis in order to be creative encouragers (Hebrews 10:24).

Praying One on One. I am a strong believer in having an "accountability partner" with whom we are accustomed to share everything – partners that know each other well, trust each other thoroughly, and commit to transparency. I have had someone like that for most of my life. The times that we have prayed together have comforted me, encouraged me, and emboldened me.

Praying with a Special Few. Sometimes there are pressing needs when you want prayer support but just from a few with whom you feel led to share.

It was 1992. A record one million students had participated in prayer at See You at the Pole. Thousands were taking advantage of the Supreme Court's ruling that allowed Christian clubs on campus. We were being interviewed about these things on national media and Christian television. Momentum was growing.

At the same time, all of us in the Network were feeling a flood of stress due to lack of financial support, increased workload, and staffing challenges. It started to affect our sense of peace and confidence. When discouragement and self-doubt began to surface in me, I asked three trusted advisors to meet me for dinner.

After listening well, they all agreed that this wasn't a management or funding problem; this was spiritual warfare. One of them said, "Think how Satan hates it when anyone prays; think how much more he hates it when a million kids pray! No wonder we've been under attack."

It turned out that the problem was "united prayer"! Ironically, the solution they proposed was more of the same. These three men committed to pray for me and the Network every day for the next thirty days. They prayed that the oppression would be removed. Then we'd talk again.

They prayed faithfully, and God seemed delighted to answer. At the beginning we were in debt, owing back rent. Thirty days later, all accounts were current, including our rent. In fact, we had a healthy balance. Two staff members had resigned in two months. A month later, one staff member announced she was returning (FYI, the other returned five years later). More importantly, we had been humbly reminded Who was in control and upon Whom we were dependent. The sense of oppression was gone.

We began to call that small group of three my "Prayer Net" – those who consistently held the net while I walked the high wire! In the year that followed, 127 others joined in. Today, thousands are committed to support the Network in prayer. Partnership in prayer, even when small, allows us to say with Paul, "On Him we have set our hope that He will continue to deliver us, as you help us by your prayers" (2 Corinthians 1:11).

Prayer Support for Specific Needs

Charles Spurgeon, the renowned British pastor, was asked about the secret of his success in light of drawing over 10,000 to hear his sermons (before electronic amplification). His clear-cut answer, "I've always had a praying people." Typically, over one hundred people were praying for him one floor below while he preached.

Even today, we have seen the atmosphere of events dramatically affected by the presence of a group of intercessors who meet privately to pray for God to work during events. The spirit of these prayer times is not just telling God what we want Him to do but looking to Him to reveal what He wants to do. It has been called "listening prayer," picturing Jesus who leads His sheep as they are attuned to Him: "My sheep listen to My voice. I know them and they follow Me" (John 10:27).

Mike Higgs, leader of a ministry called "sondance," has consistently led these prayer times for the Network and for other groups as well. What he learned about "listening prayer" as a youth pastor and network leader helped him to lead our prayer groups with an intentional focus of waiting on God in order to align with His will in united prayer. Mike speaks of seeing God at work at our national events: "I have seen thunderstorms do an about-face and head away from a huge outdoor gathering. I have seen leaders make significant, spiritually-positive changes to program plans because someone they trusted heard from God about a mid-course correction. God is always speaking if we have ears to hear."

> **"God is always speaking if we have ears to hear."**

Students also discover God's power to meet specific needs. Throughout her four years of high school, Patty met every Wednesday at 7:00 a.m. to pray with her classmates, as many as one hundred of them at times. They saw God answer prayers. She reports,

> One day we spent the entire forty-five minutes praying against violence on our campus. Sometimes there were as many as six or seven fights a day. Two days later I asked Eddie, a security guard, how he was doing. He stopped and said, "Something very strange happened yesterday. We didn't have a single fight all day on this campus." This continued for six weeks in a row! When we realized that, we rolled up our sleeves and asked, "What are we going to pray for next?"

The night before Jonathan Edwards delivered his infamous sermon, "Sinners in the Hands of an Angry God," members of the church in Enfield, Connecticut, met to pray. They were deeply burdened for God to send revival to them as part of what is now known as the First Great Awakening. They spent the whole night in prayer as did Jonathan Edwards.

The next day his sermon (though delivered in a monotone) was so anointed by the Holy Spirit that some were reported to have tightly gripped the pew in front of them for fear of slipping into a Christless eternity. Edwards issued a call for Christians to join in united prayer across New England until God visited them with revival – and, as history reveals, God did just that.

Focus on Your Jerusalem

Charity begins at home – and so should prayer. It's a biblical pattern to start where you are (Nehemiah 3, Acts 1:8). In 1857 Jeremiah Lanphier, a businessman concerned about the economic and spiritual decline around him in New York, sponsored a downtown prayer meeting. Within six months, 10,000 attended daily prayer and soon revival swept the city.

True to the biblical pattern, the most critical part of the Network is what goes on at the local level (see chapter 10). The Network in Kenosha, Wisconsin, is a tight-knit, diverse group of youth workers who share an equal commitment to each other and to reaching every student in their community. Every Thursday they gather for three hours to have lunch and pray together. Greg Stier, president of Dare 2 Share, reports about his visit to the group: "They prayed for me. They prayed for each other transparently and begged God on behalf of their teens and their towns. It was real, raw, and riveting . . . Their love for God wells up and overflows into everything else they do."

The Network is probably best known for See You at the Pole, the annual National Day of Student Prayer. It began in 1990 and each year involves one to two million youth in the U.S. and countless more in over twenty-five nations from every continent. Students meet the fourth Wednesday of September to pray for their schools, cities, and nation.

See You at the Pole (SYATP) was inspired by a small group of teenagers who gathered for a weekend retreat in Burleson, Texas. Near the end, the students' burden for their friends led them to go to three nearby schools even though it was late in the evening. They prayed for God to reach their friends and impact their schools.

At a Dallas-area leaders meeting, united prayer came up as a priority for reaching every student for Christ. The example of teenagers, both in Burleson and at other nearby schools, gave them the vision for See You at the Pole (SYATP). They circulated flyers that simply announced the basics: pray at 7 a.m., September 12, 1990, at your school's flagpole. More than 45,000 teenagers responded! Word spread throughout the Network, and in 1991 one million students gathered at schools across the nation![18] God has consistently blessed See You at the Pole. Today, it is observed by secondary schools in every state and is considered the nation's largest youth prayer event. Here are some stories of how God has blessed the humble, united prayer of our precious young people:

- **Moment of Truth.** Andrew in Topsham, Maine, was the first to arrive at the flagpole in the chill of the early morning. He had the strongest urge to pass by the pole and go to the warmth inside. But he told himself, "If God wants me to pray by myself, I will." Soon seven more joined him, then fourteen others, more Christians than most even thought were at the school!

- **Arrested for Praying.** Six teenagers in Metropolis, Illinois, prayed quietly around their flagpole before school in 1991. When the principal saw it, he called the police. Minutes later, two squad cars rolled up. They handcuffed and detained two sophomore girls and ordered adults waiting in the parking lot to disperse (including one girl's grandmother who had video-taped it all). The Network office contacted what is now the American Center for Law and Justice (ACLJ), and within a very short time the school board issued a televised apology and authorized a second SYATP gathering – one hundred attended!

- **Supported in Washington.** In the early years of SYATP, there were other instances of interference with kids who prayed before school, despite their right to do so. In 1995 the U.S. Department of Education and the President sent a directive to all public school districts underscoring the First Amendment's protection of students' freedom of religious expression, specifically citing See You at the Pole as a case in point. God can do anything! And this event paved the way for others to pray even more.

• **A Holy Hush.** The evening after SYATP was observed in Portland, Oregon, 3,000 students gathered downtown in Pioneer Square for an outdoor, citywide prayer and worship event. The coordinator, Mike Higgs, reported, "At one point, all 3,000 were kneeling in prayer and repentance. A 'holy hush' descended on the place that was supernatural. Even the large number of street kids and homeless observers became quiet." There was a sense of God's presence that touched everyone.

• **Girl Senses Prayer.** The Oklahoma City school bus unloaded very near the flagpole. As one girl stepped off the bus, the sight of the students praying stopped her in her tracks. She sat down on the curb and began to cry. A Christian teacher, who was supporting SYATP in the background, noticed her right away. Gently, she asked what was troubling her. As she wept, she pointed to the praying students and said, "Those kids . . . I feel like they're praying for me." As the conversation unfolded, the teacher helped her enter into a personal relationship with Christ right there in front of the school.

• **High Level Meeting.** A Boston elementary school girl was at her flagpole all by herself. The principal went out to ask her what she was doing. She replied, "I'm here for Meet Me at the Pole."

The principal glanced around and said, "But there is no one else here."

"Oh, no," she protested, "I'm here to meet God!"

- **Lightning-Safe.** Wisconsin was one of several states deluged with heavy thunderstorms during SYATP. Undaunted by the danger of flagpoles being lightning rods, ten brave young people prayed in a circle and wept for revival. When the thunderstorms hit Granville, Michigan, the threat of thunder and lightning made some of the students apprehensive. "Do you really think," the student leader said, "that God would call us to this time and then strike us with lightning?"

- **Does Prayer Work?** A middle schooler in Colorado Springs tells it best:

> A girl walked by us and asked what we were doing. When I told her we were praying, she got all huffy and left. But later I saw her come back and just watch us. As we walked inside, she asked if we thought prayer works. We said "Yes!" Then she told us, "When I saw you standing around the flagpole praying and not caring what others thought, I was amazed and almost overwhelmed. All I could do was stand there because I felt something was happening inside me." I told her that was God. She said, "That's what I thought, too." She asked if God would let her be a Christian. We told her He would accept her with open arms. She prayed with us right then, and we made plans to help her begin her Christian walk.

- **9/11 Response.** See You at the Pole in 2001 was one week after the tragic 9/11 attack. The theme that year, planned many months in advance, was "Desperate for God." The theme verse was Psalm 84:2, "My flesh and heart cry out to the living God." Three million teenagers turned out for SYATP that year. Several high schools had 1,000 or more. One Christian college had 2,500.

• **God in Ghana.** In Ghana, Africa, 300 young people gathered to pray. They focused their prayers on righteous living. The leader said, "The praying was intense and spontaneous. Some wept as their hearts cried out to God. Many had never experienced anything like this before."

• **From Russia with Prayer.** Fifty Russian students came together in Red Square next to Lenin's tomb. Because of the history of persecution in their country, this was the first time some had ever prayed out loud in a group.

In Jeremiah 33:3 (NASB), God says: "Call to Me, and I will answer you, and show you great and mighty things, which you do not know." Think of the multiplied impact of two million young people for whom God hears, answers, and demonstrates His mighty acts. United prayer is a powerful tool. Those who experience it will never be quite the same.

Think Globally

"Enlarge the place of your tent . . . do not hold back" (Isaiah 54:2).

That was the scriptural plea of William Carey that spawned the modern mission movement. We discussed in the last chapter how hard it was for the pastors to embrace that call. But it is a challenge for all of us to consider going beyond our borders and our comfort zones for the sake of the gospel. How can we do that?

United prayer! Praying with others about the needs of those outside of our "Jerusalem," whether it be in our own state or on another continent, paves the way for world missions.

This has been substantiated by renowned revival scholar, Dr. J. Edwin Orr. Dr. Orr also concluded, "Young people in student-led prayer bands have been at the forefront in almost every awakening."[19] One example, known as the Haystack Prayer Meeting, illustrates this so well.

In 1806, students at Williams College in Massachusetts prayed together twice a week. Seeking privacy to avoid the harassment of fellow-students, they prayed outside. A sudden downpour caused them to quickly find shelter under a haystack. One of the students, Samuel Mills, shared from a pamphlet by William Carey about the need to reach the world with the gospel. They fervently prayed together about this and were burdened to respond. Mills urged his friends, "We can do this if we will." Although these were just a few words in a haystack, God used that united prayer to spread student-led prayer and to launch the Student Volunteer Movement which would eventually send 20,000 young people to the mission field.

> Praying with others about the needs of those outside of our "Jerusalem," paves the way for world missions.

Since the year the Network started, our first long-range objective was to "help spawn a movement of God's Spirit among youth" by uniting believers to pray. That's what the apostle Paul did. He urged the church to unite in praying for him, "that God may open up a door for our message" (Colossians 4:2-4). When we pray like that, we align ourselves with God's will – and His power!

"Better Together" Questions

1. In what area of your life do you resemble the man swimming frantically to escape the shark? In that area, how does it affect your prayer to God when you are seeking to "align with His will"?

2. Are you facing something that could use the united prayer and counsel of a "special few"?

3. Who unites behind you in prayer at critical moments in your ministry or personal life? Could you engage a "Prayer Net" that would pray for you on short notice?

4. For whom are you uniting to pray locally (your city, church or community) and globally (needs beyond your borders or comfort zones)? Consider what more you might do.

Chapter 9

CONNECTED GATEKEEPERS

"May God give you a spirit of unity among yourselves . . .
so that with one heart and mouth you may glorify God"
(Romans 15:5-6).

Getting good players is easy; getting them to play together is the hard part!" Casey Stengel sums up one of his keys to success as manager of the New York Yankees' teams that won eight World Series. That's what a good network tries to do – get leaders and organizations to "play together" so that more can be accomplished as a team than could ever be accomplished by a single star player.

> A good network tries to get leaders and organizations to play together.

I'm sure that Stengel had "good players" that weren't just the "heavy hitters." He also had leaders in the clubhouse and in the office that influenced the whole team. Likewise, in the community, it is not just the heads of organizations, elected officials, or "stars" with name-recognition that need to connect. It's what some call "gatekeepers" that denotes leaders in the broader sense of the word – those who serve others (Mark 10:43).

In Bible times the gates of the city wall were a place for business, legal transactions, communication, and discussion of spiritual things. Gatekeepers were those who provided access to information and resources. They served as community elders with wisdom; they were watchmen that provided protection (Nehemiah 11:19). Today, there are gatekeepers in every ministry, organization, and community – anywhere people gather.

Convene Leaders for Common Concerns

The Network has gathered gatekeepers in countless scenarios. One day we were talking in the Network office about the challenge of getting leaders to work together. I joked that sometimes it seemed like trying to "herd cats." Fellow staff member, Kevin Boer, drawing on his days working on the family farm, said, "But that's totally possible. All you have to do is drag a big fish down the street, and they will all come running!"

The "big fish" for the Network has always been the urgency of reaching teenagers for Christ. It was that burden in 1990 which drew twenty-nine leaders to cross denominational and organizational lines for the National Youth Leaders Prayer Forum in Olive Branch, Mississippi. The agenda was to pray that God would make the 90s a "Decade of Extraordinary Prayer to Reach Young People." Planned before the first See You at the Pole event ever occurred, the meeting happened just nineteen days after it. Now, with hindsight we see that even as the gatekeepers were mustering their faith to ask God for that "big dream," He was already beginning to answer it "immeasurably more than all we ask or imagine" (Ephesians 3:20a).

Organizational labels faded and the common passion for kids united us.

As different ones shared what they were seeing in the area of prayer, including eye-witness reports from the first-ever See You at the Pole, organizational labels faded and the common passion for kids united us.

We met again the next year to continue where we left off until it became an annual event that continues today. It is called the Youth Ministry Executive Council.

Create an Environment that Encourages Harmony

Picture three adorable girls under five years old perched on a piano bench in front of the keyboard. Pointer fingers stiffly poised, they are seriously trying to make music together. I have that picture! But I didn't hear the sounds that went with it. Their grandparents told me I didn't miss a thing. "It was loud, but no harmony was achieved, either musically or relationally." Harmonizing doesn't just happen.

Maybe you can remember when there wasn't much cooperation between denominations, when parachurch ministries judged each other because of different ministry approaches, and when materials didn't get used unless one's own ministry label was on them. Hopefully, that's a *distant* memory for you! Though differences of opinion are expected and staying in tune with each other will always take work, there is much more inter-ministry collaboration going on these days. Steve Douglass, President of Cru, observed, "I can remember when there was not a high degree of unity in the body of Christ in the U.S. But things have changed. Now there is a great deal of willingness to help and serve other organizations."[20]

Former missionary society leader, Dr. Wesley Duewel, tells how their early discoveries about unity made a huge difference in India. One missionary had been praying earnestly day after day for God to send revival to the work he was doing. But every time he prayed, the Spirit brought to his mind another missionary with whom he had a serious disagreement. Finally, out of conviction, he traveled to the other missionary's town. When he knocked on the door, he fell to his knees and started asking the surprised missionary for forgiveness. But the other missionary interrupted, "I am the one who needs to ask your forgiveness." A sweet time of reconciliation followed.

As they prayed in unity, each asked God to send revival to the other's work. They began working together. Within twelve months both churches experienced the revival for which they had been praying. Dr. Duewel observed, "We cannot prevail in prayer while disunity festers. As much as it is in our power, we must seek to humble ourselves, take the blame, and restore unity" (Matthew 5:23-24, Romans 12:18). [21]

Hopefully, we can learn from that example of courageously taking the initiative to mend a broken relationship. But we can also learn the value of being proactive, if possible, in order to pave the way to "live in harmony with one another" (Romans 12:16).

The Network's annual meeting of the Youth Ministry Executive Council (YMEC), mentioned above, convenes presidents of national youth organizations and denominations to pray and communicate together over a two-day period. In addition to hearing from each other on issues of common concern, having time over meals and recreation helps to build relationships and provide a safe place for deeper sharing.

Mike Calhoun spoke to me of his experience attending YMEC and representing Word of Life Fellowship:

> The first time I came to YMEC, I was familiar with many of the names of the leaders of the major student ministries, but I hardly knew any of them. I wondered, "How will I fit in and will it be worth my time and investment?" The answer has been a resounding "Yes!" for more than fifteen years. Our entire global   ministry has benefited greatly from my interaction with these leaders on vision, insight, and training, not to mention the networking with the decision makers from other organizations. But even more important was that some of these leaders became my close friends. They shared my same passion. We laughed, cried, and prayed together. Some have become significant prayer partners in times of my greatest, personal challenges. I am eternally grateful that I have this team of exceptional friends.

David Blair, the representative of Church of God, Cleveland, explains further about how unity is built:

> At YMEC I feel the ground is level no matter who is in the room. It's an open environment where we as   leaders share

in worship, fellowship, and the Word of God, but we can also share our struggles and hurts. Some revolutionary initiatives, events, and programs have naturally emerged, just because of the chemistry of these leaders being together. (My wife loves for me to attend because she says that I come home energized, spiritually challenged, and motivated!)

Jay Mooney reflected back on his experiences at YMEC as representative of the Assemblies of God: "I love coming together. It's a way of seeing what is going on 'above the fence line' as opposed to looking through a knot hole in the fence. It gives me a perspective on the variety of ways to do ministry – and ours is one way."

When Romans 12:16 speaks of living in harmony, it is based on the idea of being "in tune" with each other. Some versions translate it, "Be of the same mind toward one another." This doesn't mean having the same opinion; it means being humble about your opinion (Romans 12:16b), so that you can really listen to the other person.

If that's how harmony works, it requires us to be in the same place at the same time. Some gatekeepers never connect with each other because of stereotypes and assumptions. There's nothing like spending extended time together to start getting in tune with each other by sharing meals, having fun, and praying together about ministry and personal challenges. Satan wants to keep us apart, but when we come together, we can see why. When there's harmony, the world takes note (John 17:21)!

Set the Stage for Creativity

God seldom gives a great idea to just one person. He usually entrusts it to a number of people who will come at it from different angles. Then, He weaves it all together to accomplish His purpose. The first time I saw this, it intimidated me (see chapter 3). But since it now occurs so often, the "light goes on" whenever it happens. We can tell that God is up to something.

I remember being at a meeting in Singapore where a leader of a youth network in Finland described his vision for an event that sounded exactly like something we had recently done in the U.S. When I inquired about it, he said he had never heard of our event, but he would love to know how we did it. That was the beginning of a wonderful partnership.

> How should we marshal the resources He has given us?

When we gather with others representing different streams of God's work, we need to expect this pattern and welcome it when someone echoes the vision God has given us. Ecclesiastes 1:9-10 reminds us that "there is nothing new under the sun." This is the way God will generate momentum to accomplish His will. We don't want to get in the way by worrying about who thought of it first.

When we have that spirit, it changes the nature of gatekeeper meetings. If you have a mix of perspectives and resources and are not worried about whose label is on it or who gets the credit, it's amazing what progress can be made on challenging issues. We can roll up our sleeves and ask God for His wisdom about what to do; then, listen together for His leading about how we should marshal the resources He has given us (2 Chronicles 20).

- **To reach the campus.** The Network has brought as many as sixty ministries together at different times to plan how to establish ministries to every school, to define what it means to "reach a campus," to create unique materials to facilitate those goals, and ultimately to set up an ongoing ministry called Campus Alliance.

- **To focus on cities.** Ministries like the Urban Youth Worker Institute have worked together with the Network to convene leaders to address the evolving needs and uniqueness of networking in urban areas. With gatekeepers present who represented different ethnicities, we found increased creativity, resources, and motivation to form strategies and structures that were beyond what could have happened individually.

• **To address youth leaving the church.** What do we do in the face of the terrible statistics about youth who leave the church and don't return? The collaboration of response touched almost every college ministry and turned into a full-time effort called Youth Transition Network.

• **To mobilize younger leaders.** There is a movement to involve younger leaders in ministry, not just younger adults but children. As gatekeepers gather, we are more apt to think outside the box about the big picture. In so doing, we discovered the 4/14 Window Global Initiative — a movement that is mobilizing children ages four to fourteen to utilize their gifts to help fulfill the Great Commission. This expands the parameters of traditional youth ministry. We celebrate it and seek to integrate with it.

Collaborate – As the Spirit Leads You

We live at a time when we can't afford the luxury of proceeding without urgency or by going solo.

Peter reminds us that our eternal perspective should lead us to live by priorities: to pray, love deeply, be hospitable, and to serve one another according to our gifts (1 Peter 4:7-10). So gathering as gatekeepers gives us that opportunity, and we should take seriously what God prompts us to do in collaboration and support of one another.

At Schools. Youth pastors in Costa Mesa, California, prayed for ways to minister at area schools. The regional director of the Christian Educators Association, Forrest Turpen, and the regional coordinator of

> We live at a time when we can't afford the luxury of ... going solo.

the National Network of Youth Ministries, Mike DeVito, partnered to provide a means to serve the needs of area high schools by doing physical makeovers on every campus. Hundreds of church volunteers were involved, and there was great appreciation from school leadership.

No Logos. Jay Mooney of Assemblies of God said, "It's important for our denomination to network within the larger body of Christ . . . If there is something we have that will help them, I am glad to offer it for their use, even if they are not part of my denomination and even if they don't carry our logo." Fellowship of Christian Athletes acted on that premise as well. When the FCA president shared at YMEC about their successful drug use prevention program, he offered the complete program to anyone who wanted to use it even if they wanted to print it under their own ministry name.

Joining Forces. One of the crisis areas gatekeepers have discussed recently is how to combat the bombardment of our youth culture with a secular and immoral world view. The Network has enjoyed a long partnership with Josh McDowell, who has passionately worked on this for fifty years. We also know that Morality in Media, another fifty-year-old ministry, leads campaigns to enforce pornography laws and to provide resources to promote internet safety. These two ministries were not even aware of the overlap and had never met each other. It was our privilege to connect these two gatekeepers. As a result of discovering common ground, they have collaborated in the resources they offer and have coordinated strategies to unite their efforts and multiply their impact.

"If you want to go fast, go alone;
if you want to go far, go together." (African Proverb)

Networking is needed at all levels, but when you network the gate-keepers, you create an environment in each constituency that is more open to cooperation and collaboration. While evidence may show that we are "better together," it is not a foregone conclusion among ministry leaders. For years the tendency has been to "go alone," but the needs of our ministries and the crisis of our culture are moving the pendulum toward "going together." And it makes sense.

My former neighbor is a highly-skilled stone mason. If you looked at his finished work, you would be impressed. But one critical yet visible part of his end product usually went completely unnoticed – the mortar. Without it he would only have a stack of rocks or bricks. One stone can be attractive alone, but it isn't until we find a way to cement them together that we can build something significant. That's the value of connecting the gatekeepers. Each ministry has value, but God didn't intend for us to do ministry alone. He wants us to work together in "complete unity." When the mortar of unity cements us together, we will be a testimony to the world that God loves them and wants them to believe in His Son, Jesus (John 17:21-23).

"Better Together" Questions

1. What is the "big fish" that would draw gatekeepers together in your area of greatest concern?

2. Is it possible that progress is being hindered because you are not in harmony with another leader? What can you do to restore unity?

3. Is God prompting you to collaborate with someone else, using your gifts and /or resources?

4. What is the "mortar" in your life and ministry that motivates you to "go together" instead of "go alone"? Do you need to find more "mortar"?

Chapter 10

GRASSROOTS IMPACT

C hrist's Great Commission would have been pointless if believers throughout the ages didn't act on it. Scripture is full of incredible promises and principles, but the intention is that we "be doers of the word, and not hearers only" (James 1:22, NKJV). That action must start in each of us *individually*, and as we connect with other "doers," we begin to make an impact – "in Jerusalem, and in all Judea and Samaria, and to the ends of the earth" (Acts 1:8).

That is true of the principles in this book. As strongly as I feel about the value of each principle and the truth in each chapter, it really doesn't mean much to believe that we are "better together" until it turns into convictions that affect you and me where we live.

> It really doesn't mean much to believe that we are "better together" until it turns into convictions that affect you and me where we live.

Yes, the Network was born in meetings of national leaders who had a vision of uniting to reach youth. But once it was formed, the immediate response was to take the covenant and objectives back home to discuss and apply locally with fellow workers. In the next year, individual members began to sign up, receiving help to disciple students, and to begin focusing on the goal to reach every high school. Within six years (1987), there were local networks with coordinators established in cities, making up over fifty percent of the nation's youth.[22]

See You at the Pole has made a worldwide impact (see chapter 8), but it started locally with a goal to reach local schools. Picture that small group of youth workers, sitting around the table in Texas and discussing that student involvement in outreach and prayer were the keys to reaching every school. These adults united out of mutual concern, first, for their "Jerusalem."

The concern for every person's "home base" is still at the heart of the Network. Now there are networks in every state and a majority of communities. Over the years, our local coordinators have found that there are four priorities that, when observed, will pave the way for positive impact in communities.

PRAY TOGETHER – Aligning with God's Will

When Jesus explained who He was to people in the temple, He said, "I do nothing on My own but speak just what the Father has taught Me . . . I always do what pleases Him" (John 8:28-29). If that was Jesus' way of determining His direction, how much more should we be sure we depend on God for ours!

Mike Higgs (referenced in chapter 8) said, "As a youth pastor, I had a hazardous tendency to make great plans and ask God to bless them, rather than to ask Him for *His plans* and expect Him to answer!" But Mike learned to recognize that tendency and led his fellow network members in Portland, Oregon, to make their plans in a way that looked to God for His will and His leadings. He said, "We had a dozen youth worker networks in our city. We transitioned from just asking Him to bless our plans and became more intentional about waiting on God for His marching orders and His directives in our prayer times." Waiting on the Lord together is an act of unity. It increases our sensitivity to His will and fills us with expectation and strength because our hope is in the

Everlasting God rather than ourselves (Isaiah 40:28-31).

Sherri went to Youth Congress '85 (co-sponsored by the Network) and returned to Wichita committed to reach her school for Christ. She started a campus Bible study, and by the end of the school year, it multiplied student-led campus Bible studies to all eight city schools. Today, served by Keith Malcom and the Campus Ministry Network, there are forty student-led campus Bible studies in virtually every secondary school in the greater Wichita area.

Student-led prayer is also part of this movement – not only at See You at the Pole but also in schools. One campus prayer group meets every Wednesday in the choir room. Group members ask fellow students to write down their prayer requests during the week and place them in Mason jars which get filled to overflowing! Then, on Wednesday morning each request gets prayed for privately. They gather at the end to pray together for the school as a whole. When they leave, each prayer request gets taken home for prayer throughout the week.

> **Waiting on the Lord together is an act of unity.**

The impact upon the school has been subtle but definite. The prayer group has been around long enough that it is not the subject of ridicule. Instead, students often show up in the choir room asking for prayer or just to listen in.

BUILD RELATIONSHIPS – Loving Each Other

We need each other! From creation God told us that we weren't meant to go through life alone (Genesis 2:18). It's the nature of the body of Christ to be connected – to share deeply in one another's joys and hardships, to be devoted to them (1 Corinthians 12:25-26, Romans 12:10).

That was truly the spirit of the Cincinnati Network. It was time for prayer at their monthly meeting – a highlight for these friends who loved the opportunity to pray together about their lives and ministries. When they got around to the youth worker who hosted the meeting, he dropped his head and poured out his heart.

This young man was extremely gifted, popular with his students, and loved by his church. His voice broke as he shared anxiously, "As you know, I'm a newlywed. My wife resents this church, the ministry, and even the attention I give to students." He continued in more detail. Suffice it to say, he was really hurting.

Keith Krueger, the Network coordinator, confessed, "We were all stunned! We dropped everything on the agenda and just focused on him. We listened, loved him, and gathered around to pray. But our counsel was straightforward, 'It would be better for you and your students to leave the ministry than to lose your marriage.'"

Within a month he made that announcement. He was leaving youth ministry, and he and his wife would return to their hometown to rebuild their marriage and wait on the Lord. Keith realized, "There is a healthy network where he is moving, and the coordinator is a good friend of mine. Little did I know that the coordinator was also close to the family of the youth worker's wife."

A few years later Keith visited that city to speak to a group of youth workers. There he was, a glowing face on the front row! He and his family had been loved and cared for. He was now serving in another church as a youth pastor – this time, with the full blessing and involvement of his precious wife. Their whole perspective on ministry and the local church had changed. Keith was so thrilled. He said, "We hugged, and that said it all! Don't you marvel at the blessing of the body of Christ when it is working together?"

Scripture says: "How good and pleasant it is when God's people live together in unity" (Psalm 133:1)! In this "high tech" world when many prefer social media over face-to-face interaction, we need meaningful personal relationships more than ever. The apostle Paul said he had such joy when he saw believers "united in spirit, intent on one purpose" (Philippians 2:2, NASB). There's no substitute for someone's arm around your shoulder or seeing eye to eye with another or getting a pat on the back.

Strong one-on-one relationships are a primary ingredient, and probably the favorite one, for effective cooperation. Jim Burns, veteran youth speaker and trainer, said, "One of the reasons there is such a quick turnover in youth work is because many people never join forces with other like-minded youth workers . . . I remember my first community network as a youth pastor. Some of the interactions we had were life-changing. Many of these people are still some of my closest friends."[23]

DEVELOP STRATEGIES – Impacting Others

Listening is a big part of developing networking strategies. As we've seen above, the first two priorities both require a sensitive heart:

- Prayer involves seeking to know God's will (Matthew 6:9-10).
- Relationships are based on sensitivity to each other (James 1:19).

If we have done those two things well, then developing strategies takes on a new dimension. God guides our plans and gives us His perspective which spans "all generations" (Psalm 33:11).

When the idea of networking started to catch on at the grassroots, we saw God provide volunteers to coordinate city networks – 122 by 1988. Membership had tripled in the three years prior to that, and we were praying for God to give us more leaders. A few years later, I was standing with Doug Clark, the Network's director of field ministries, looking at the U.S. map that was divided up into Network regions. Though I can't remember all the details, I do remember how we were both impressed at the same time that God was in the process of raising up "salaried coordinators" who would be able to invest more time in the work. It was an insight that changed our thinking about the future.

God is accustomed to speaking to us through others (Proverbs 11:14). Successful local networks are built on identifying needs, resources, and the actions required to move forward. In the Midwest, regional Network coordinators did "Listen and Learn Tours," traveling to each coordinator's community to better understand the needs of their youth, youth workers, and local networks. That assessment was the basis for their planning.

For the coordinator in Sioux Falls, South Dakota, that assessment helped shape a city-reaching strategy which produced multiple networks, tailored to the needs of youth in area neighborhood churches and ministries. For the rural coordinator in Iowa, the Listening Tour inspired him to form a network of five youth pastors plus the local FCA director to start campus ministries in a four-city rural area. The initiative expanded to begin networks in three other rural areas.

Sometimes we don't get the opportunity to plan ahead. In those times we are thankful if we have something like a network in our lives to undergird us with support. David Grant, youth pastor and network coordinator in Irving, Texas, told me how his network navigated a community tragedy.

A popular senior from a high school near David's church went missing after cliff diving, and he was feared dead. Hundreds of students gathered at the football stadium to pray and honor his memory. During the heavy counseling of the next few days, people were gaining closure only to learn that another senior at the same high school had just taken his life. It was a grueling, grief-stricken time for everyone.

> "Although the week had been exhausting, I observed the simple and beautiful truth that I didn't have to walk through that week alone."

David said, "Although the week had been exhausting, I observed the simple and beautiful truth that I didn't have to walk through that week alone."

The youth worker network provided a means for supporting each other. They pulled together on the first night to plan how they could respond and help. In grief counseling they worked like a triage team, each playing a role to comfort students flooded with emotions. They were together at the memorial service, too.

One youth pastor wrote David about his thankfulness for the network at a time of crisis. "I am humbled to have linked arms to serve our God by serving our community together. I am blown away at the reality that WE ARE BETTER TOGETHER. I often get so caught up in my weekly stuff that I neglect building relationships with those doing the same things in the same town. Forgive me."

David said, "There is power in churches and youth workers serving together with one heart. I don't know how we would have dealt with the tragedies if youth workers were not willing and eager to work and pray together. I'm so thankful there was a great level of trust and relationship before all this went down and even more thankful for the deepening of those relationships that resulted."

Though each of the above examples is very relational in nature, those relationships were enhanced by a simple support structure that was operating behind the scenes. "Effective, lasting partnerships need a committed facilitator – someone who, by consensus, has been given the role of bringing the partnership to life and keeping the fires burning. He is one who demonstrates patience, tenacity, vision and the spirit of a servant."[24] This may be similar to what Jesus calls "a person of peace" (Matthew 10:5-7) who is known and trusted in the community and who opens the door to involve others.

In the Network, this is the coordinator. But he doesn't work alone. The pattern is for him to be supported by a team of fellow leaders who share responsibilities, and, if needed, transition into greater leadership when change inevitably comes to the group. This leadership team helps keep the focus on the primary goals and objectives in a way that captures the imagination and motivation of the group and is relevant to each partner.[25]

Mike DeVito reminded me of his first experience in our network here in San Diego: "Being part of the Network made me part of something bigger than myself. It stimulated vision and passion I didn't have and maybe never would have had. When you asked me to help, I saw a place for my gifts and talents. It gave me more confidence. Networking made me better!"

SHARE RESOURCES – Multiplying Effectiveness

Resources aren't just books, videos and stuff you buy at a store – or even all that is available on the internet. Traditional resources are still essential. But in the networking world, the greatest resources are people – those who share your vision, businesses, or ministries, those who work in a related field, leaders who are connected to funding, ideas, and infrastructure. Networking links one or more of these elements in your sphere of influence. In so doing, you not only serve each other but also multiply your outcomes. It can get pretty exciting (1 Peter 4:10)!

High school students from the Long Beach, California, area met early in the morning each week. Though from different schools, they had the same heart – to live for Christ on their campuses. Local youth workers from the Network met with them to listen, to encourage, and to help. Al Siebert and his staff from Long Beach Youth for Christ began to talk with the other youth workers in the Network about how to respond to the students' need for help in learning how to reach out to their friends. They all agreed to sponsor a training event called "Turn Your Campus." About 200 attended that first event, challenging kids to be "salt and light" (Matthew 5:13-15) and to see their campus as their place of ministry. That was over twenty years ago. The event was so well received by students, youth workers, and educators that it has been repeated annually. It is now co-sponsored by six ministries and draws over 1,600 students.

Youth mission leaders found common ground to share successes and challenges at the Network's national events. As a result, youth mission agencies set out to meet some of the needs that surfaced through unprecedented collaboration. They focused on the need to establish standards for short term mission trips. They also created a strategy to help students avoid the common pitfalls that occur when participants in mission trips return home, and they are unable to apply what they learned. The Youth Missions Network helped to convene gatherings focused on developing the Standards of Excellence for Short Term Missions (SOE) and designing "The Next Mile" materials that provide comprehensive training for participants, beginning before they leave and continuing long after they return. Both of these resources are good examples of addressing local needs in ways that have benefited the entire nation.[26]

The Reach Youth New England Network, under the leadership of Mark Orr, has found a resource that many cities in their region use to identify with world hunger and to initiate help. World Vision's "30 Hour Famine" was the vehicle that kids used to raise funds while they personally fasted for thirty hours. After four years of participation, 1,500 kids and leaders have raised over $200,000!

The Network has seen the youth culture morph and change in many ways over the years. The target audience has continued moving to younger ages. A thriving, international initiative has emerged. It is called "The 4/14 Window Movement," and it focuses on children ages four to fourteen. Their plan is not only to reach those children but also to mobilize them in ministry.

Here's how one church responded to that need and prompted a movement that spread to other churches:

When Clint May served as children's pastor at Wedgwood Baptist Church in Fort Worth, Texas, he made an amazing discovery that attracted a network of other churches. He found that grade schoolers could go on mission trips to challenging areas just like adults. With proper advance training, kids did all the speaking, all the witnessing, formed praise bands and led the activities. The result was large numbers of children giving their lives to Christ. Many churches throughout the area joined in under the banner "Leaders in Training." Together, they have mobilized more than 250 trained children, impacting their entire city. Now the idea is spreading to other states. Clint says, "Every year adult leaders return from our student mission trips in amazement of what the Lord is doing . . . to empower children to fulfill the Great Commission." This is just one expression of what is becoming an international movement of children in ministry.

Expand Your Circle

The premise that we are "better together" is well substantiated, but its significance goes far beyond the exhilaration of the experience. Its potential to impact the world begins with seeing results right where we live. Many networks limit involvement to a small circle of like-minded people. But if we were to expand our scope, we would most likely find a vast resource of people who share our vision and concerns – maybe not exactly, but there would be overlapping benefits. For instance, we have found that youth workers are not the only ones who care about teenagers. Teachers, coaches, social workers, business leaders, senior pastors, parents, and many others are equally committed to youth.

Like Nehemiah and all the families who rebuilt Jerusalem's wall, think of the impact we could have if we would cooperate to meet the needs of our communities "with the help of our God" (Nehemiah 6:15-16)!

"Better Together" Questions

1. *Prayer* – Does the group with whom you network really "wait on God" for His leading about what to do? Or is praying together more like a punctuation mark in a long sentence of others' opinions?

2. *Relationships* – Do you get enough face time with people you know and trust? Beside your immediate family, who are you deeply connected with in the body of Christ?

3. *Strategy* – What needs is your network trying to meet? What needs are they meeting for you?

4. *Resources* – Who else is there in your community that also cares deeply about some aspect of what your network is trying to accomplish? What about connecting with them – at least for communication purposes?

Chapter 11

SUSTAINED FOCUS

Even the Lone Ranger had Tonto. They discovered that their chances for survival were much better if they were a team. In ministry, we weren't meant to be Lone Rangers either.

When Jesus sent his disciples out, he sent them out two by two (Luke 10:1). Why? Maybe it's because they wouldn't go one by one!

Ministry is very rewarding, but often it is very hard. My positive-thinking friends would say it's "challenging" – yes, but frankly, it can be down-right grueling!

> In ministry, we weren't meant to be Lone Rangers.

Willing to Commit for a Lifetime

The challenges may be especially eye-opening for people in youth ministry who are young, energetic, and perhaps fresh out of school. When the Network began, youth work was viewed as "entry-level" ministry – a transitional job on the way "up" to being a senior pastor. What's more, look at all the fun you could have playing with kids! But on average a youth minister's "bag of tricks" usually ran out in about six to nine months. Very few saw youth ministry as a profession. The founders of the Network felt this had to be one of the components of the covenant

> I often wonder where I would be today if those people had not prayed for me and believed in me when they did.

we committed to (see Appendix 1): "A willingness to minister to youth for a lifetime, should God so direct."

Diane Brask was one of those fresh, energetic, visionary young leaders. During her senior year of college God called her to a lifetime of ministry. She didn't expect it would be to youth, but God clearly directed her to go back to her home to lead a rural youth ministry. It wasn't where or what she pictured, but as God immersed her in ministry, He gave her a heart for lost students and for helping kids grow in their faith. She learned that if people networked, they could reach far more teenagers for Christ than by working alone. She was seeing progress toward her vision of a movement for Christ that would impact schools – that is until, as she describes it . . .

On one horrible, unforgettable day it seemed to be all over. I experienced a vicious attack of accusations from Satan aimed at destroying me, my ministry, and the vision of churches uniting to reach students for Christ. It was a day from hell – the beginning of the darkest season of my life. I felt like I was finished.

Had it not been for the support of the Network, I think I would have thrown in the towel. Network leaders from several different areas became a safety net for me to keep me from going under. Their phone calls, notes, emails, and visits conveyed their love and prayers for me in a way that brought healing and hope.

They believed God was not finished with me. Once I saw God provide resolution at home, He actually expanded my ministry! The Network asked me to be their "rural voice" with a focus on reaching and supporting youth in smaller communities across America. I never dreamed of that. Since then, my ministry has expanded to people in rural communities all over the world! I often wonder where I would be today if those people had not prayed for me and believed in me when they did.

Keeping Aligned with True North

Diane felt that God called her to a lifetime of serving Him in ministry. She made a commitment to follow Him anywhere. She was full of anticipation until He showed her that He wanted her to minister in her very small, very rural hometown.

She burst into tears. She had envisioned going to "the ends of the earth" (Acts 1:8), but it felt like a dead end. She had a decision to make. Later she endured a heavy trial. Finally, she was given the opportunity to restart with an even broader scope. Each time she had to make a decision, sometimes with a little help from her friends, she stayed true to God's leading.

Did He change His mind?

Did He bait and switch?

No. God is our North Star, our point of reference for staying on course. He doesn't change (Malachi 3:6). But as with ships navigating in the high seas, we don't always see the North Star clearly. The compass made it possible to always know the direction of "true north." However, due to the changing magnetic pull of the earth, compasses need to be adjusted every few years. If not, they will become inaccurate and potentially dangerous.

> God is our North Star, our point of reference for staying on course.

So it is with following the Lord's leading. It shouldn't surprise us that there are changes. We may need to adjust. None of us can understand where God's calling may lead us in the long run. That's why He longs for us to seek Him daily (Psalm 5:2-3). When things don't look right, we look to Him to see if it's time for an adjustment. In 2 Chronicles 20, Jehoshaphat got the news that a "vast army" was coming to attack. His first response was to call the people together to "seek Him." He prayed (v. 12), "We do not know what to do, but our eyes are on You." God's unorthodox yet miraculous response shows the wisdom of trusting His leading and not our own notions (See 2 Chronicles 20:13).

Most of us don't like change, but the world is changing fast whether we like it or not. Even the Network has transitioned. After serving as president for over twenty-eight years, I felt God showed me that it was time to pass the baton to another leader. After a prayerful search, God led the board to select T. Ray Grandstaff, a gifted and godly man. Despite his leadership and innovations, especially his Communities of Hope strategy, the global, economic downturn took a serious toll on the Network's resources. Some staff had to be released and, by mutual consent, that included our new CEO. It was a heart-breaker. We loved T. Ray, but God revealed no other options.

This was the time for everyone to seek God's direction like Jehoshaphat. It was a time to be brutally honest, to assess our needs, resources, and priorities. Had God taken His hand off the Network? Off of T. Ray? No! But He wanted us to adjust our focus, to realign our plans, and to enter into greater dependency on Him.

Not Derailed by Adversity

When we are right in the middle of the battle, sustaining our focus gets complicated. It's hard not to be distracted, even overwhelmed, when all the flak is flying (Ephesians 6:16). That's why we need each other, why Diane needed her safety net, and Network leadership needed to huddle together to seek God about what to do when the bottom fell out.

Bill Koontz was a natural leader. As a youth pastor, he attended one of the Network's first Forums and immediately aligned with the vision. He started the first network in Cincinnati, and within a few years began connecting with other leaders to launch networks elsewhere. The groundwork was laid for a statewide network. Momentum was really building.

Then came the devastating news that Bill's wife of twelve years had filed for divorce. Bill remembers, "The heartache of a fractured marriage and its fallout on my two children was nearly unbearable."

He felt he should resign from his church youth ministry – deepening his sadness. Unknown to Bill, God had begun to put people in place to help sustain him. Keith Krueger had just moved to Cincinnati the year before the divorce. He and Bill had struck a friendship at the first Forum so they were in contact. The year after the divorce, Keith insisted that Bill come to that year's Forum, despite the way he was feeling. Bill sees more clearly now: "Keith knew that this was a time when he and the Network could serve me, to help bind up my wounds. In fact, we had arranged to spend a couple of extra days together. I bathed in the worship, messages, and prayer. The Network was part of what God used to bring healing to my broken heart."

God continued to use Keith in Bill's life to encourage and help him re-build and renew. Bill remarried and Keith helped tie the knot. Bill continues in business, no longer in full-time church ministry, but you might not know it at first glance. He found his niche as an active layman in his local church where he started ministries for senior high students and for those in need of help with pre-marital counseling, divorce recovery, marriage enrichment, and stewardship. Bill reflects, "I am so thankful for Keith and the Network for linking arms with me through my darkness . . . for the part they played in turning my mourning into gladness."

We praise God for the victories, but our hearts go out to each one for all the pain and hardships they endured. No one would wish those things on anyone. But those of us who read this can see how God sustained them, how He used the body of Christ, and how it was worth it to stay faithful. 2 Corinthians 4:6-10 explains:

> For God, who said, "Let light shine out of darkness," made his light shine in our hearts to give us the light of the knowledge of God's glory displayed in the face of

Christ. But we have this treasure in jars of clay to show that this all-surpassing power is from God and not from us.

We are hard-pressed on every side, but not crushed; perplexed, but not in despair; persecuted, but not abandoned; struck down, but not destroyed. We always carry around in our body the death of Jesus, so that the life of Jesus may also be revealed in our body.

Persevering Without Losing Heart

You've read how Keith Krueger and his network have been an integral help for fellow youth workers, but there was a time when this "pastor to pastors" needed pastoring. Keith taught others about how much Satan targets those who give their lives to reach youth. But the target was on his back, too.

Keith had moved from another state to follow the vision of the pastor who planted his church. As his youth pastor, they would see God develop it into a church that planted other churches. But this good and godly man, who was now Keith's close friend, became a victim of wrong choices that forced him to leave the church. The pastor was so deeply wounded that he left the ministry altogether.

The whole church was in upheaval, torn by division and heartache. Keith was a good youth pastor, seeing a lot of fruit, but in that situation he couldn't do his job. The crisis at church immobilized him. Keith shared:

> I was personally entwined in the life of the church. My spirit was crushed by the turn of events, and I couldn't function. I was in tears constantly. I was so distraught in my spirit that I thought I was losing control.
>
> To be honest, I was ready to quit! Without the vision and care of fellow youth workers, I would not be in ministry today. God used those servants to speak Scriptures into my life, comfort me, and challenge me to take my eyes off my pastor and friend and to remember the calling of the Savior.

Keith reminded me of my personal visit to him. I arranged for a stop-over in his city when traveling on Network business. Keith poured out his heart. He said he felt like he had fallen in a pit and couldn't get out. He told me later, "You gently counseled me, reminded me of my call and helped me out of the pit by urging me to continue in the strength of the Lord. That was a pivotal day in my life as a youth worker."

I had *no idea* of the impact of our conversation and prayers. I didn't feel like I did anything special. But it is a good reminder to me of how God can use us, beyond our expectation, as we are willing to "carry each other's burdens" (Galatians 6:2) and "come alongside to comfort" (2 Corinthians 1:4). The good news is that Keith has continued faithfully in ministry and serves today as an elder in that church.

Ministry can be rigorous, but remember, God's purpose for us is not to make ministry stress-free.

Ministry can be rigorous, but remember, God's purpose for us is not to make ministry stress-free. James 1:2-4 tells us that we should expect trials, testing of our faith, and the need to persevere. We should even "consider it all joy" because God's end goal for us is that we will "be mature and complete" in Christ.

As we have seen in the examples above, we are more likely to sustain our focus on God's goal for us if we "join together . . . every part doing its share" so that we "grow to maturity" in Christ (Ephesians 4: 15-16).

"Better Together" Questions

1. Who is your "Tonto," the one who will keep you from being a "Lone Ranger"? Who is that person who believes in you and will stick with you in your life's vision?

2. Are you staying on God's "true north" for you? Or does your "compass" need to be realigned in some areas to allow for the changes in your life?

3. What "valleys" (adversities) in your life threaten to derail your vision? Who is your safety net, and how are they helping you?

4. Is God prompting you to take some action to "come alongside to comfort" or encourage someone?

Chapter 12

SPIRIT-EMPOWERED UNITY

Uncle Max lowered the basketball hoop for his two-year-old nephew who desperately wanted to make a basket. The little tyke tried his best to throw that big orb, one-third his size, toward the hoop. Finally, Uncle Max scooped him up with the ball – all the way to the rim – so that he could "stuff the basket" like a seven-footer. His nephew squealed with delight, "All by myself!"[27]

That is so like human nature, isn't it? It is so exhilarating to be at the center of accomplishing something big! It is easy to underplay that it was the Father who lifted us up, guided our hands, and made our success possible. If we keep thinking that way, it isn't long before we start thinking we really can do slam dunks "all by myself."

In ministry, when things get "grueling" (as mentioned in the last chapter), most of us just press on, which is usually a good quality. But sometimes we start to depend on ourselves to do the "slam dunks," and we don't even realize it. Like Samson with his hair cut (Judges 16:17-22), our spiritual power leaves us, and all we can do is what we can do in our own strength. Some may have more natural abilities than others, but in time we lose our joy and our effectiveness (Psalm 32:1-4).

There's a reason the last chapter of this book is about Spirit-empowered unity. As much as the previous eleven principles can stand alone, none of them can deliver the kind of supernatural unity we want unless we have the Holy Spirit's power. I think Jesus emphasized the unity of believers in his last prayer before the cross because He knew how difficult and yet important it would be (Ephesians 4:3). It would be the means of protecting us from Satan's power (John 17:15) and the way the world would believe in Jesus and in God's love for us (John 17:23).

It is wonderful to know that Jesus wants us to be united with each other, and even more wonderful to know that He wants us to be united with Him and God, His Father. But this kind of unity is only possible because of the gift Jesus spoke of in the previous chapter – the gift of the Holy Spirit (John 16:7-16).

Experiencing God's Power Personally

Dave Busby, who died in 1997 of cystic fibrosis, was a beloved speaker at Network events who impacted millions of students and youth workers about their walks with God. At a Network regional conference, Dave spoke on "The Active Presence of God in Ministry." Never known for subtlety, Dave alluded to his impression that many ministries might not even notice if the Holy Spirit's power was removed. There were a few chuckles, until unexpectedly he asked, "What are you doing in ministry that could only be explained by the power of God?"

"What are you doing in ministry that could only be explained by the power of God?"

There was an awkward silence. How would you answer?

If we are to demonstrate God's power, we must be certain that we are personally experiencing the control of the Holy Spirit in our daily lives. "What we have received is not the spirit of the world, but the Spirit who is from God, so that we may understand what God has freely given us" (1 Corinthians 2:12). Receiving the Spirit of God is about being filled with the Holy Spirit – continually confessing our sins (1 John 1:9) and surrendering to the Spirit's control according to His command (Ephesians 5:18) and His promise (1 John 5:14-15).[28] That paves the way for the exciting adventure of discovering "what the will of the Lord is" (Ephesians 5: 15, 17) through prayer, Bible study, and wise counsel.

Once we have the confidence that we are individually filled with the Spirit and that He is guiding our unity, it sets the stage for seeing and demonstrating God's power.

One pastor, who was part of the Welsh Revival in 1904-1905, observed, "When we find harmony with God, we begin to find harmony with one another." After witnessing revival in another church, he began fervently praying for revival in his own church. "Slowly signs began . . . People in the church who had taken offense with each other were reconciled. Unity prepared the way of the Lord."[29]

Think of the power of unity when it is directed by God! A.W. Tozer explains it with this vivid picture: "Has it ever occurred to you that one hundred pianos all tuned to the same fork are automatically tuned to each other? They are of one accord by being tuned, not to each other, but . . . each one looking away to Christ, is in heart nearer to each other than they could possibly be if they turn their eyes away from God to strive for closer fellowship."[30]

> "Has it ever occurred to you that one hundred pianos all tuned to the same fork are automatically tuned to each other?"

Letting God's Spirit Lead us Together

How do we get in tune with the Lord like that?

It starts with an open heart that is yielded to God's moving through us as He wills. Like the geyser seeking a place to erupt in Yellowstone Park, God waits for broken ground where He can pour out His power and blessing. "The sacrifices of God are a broken spirit; a broken and a contrite heart, O God, You will not despise" (Psalm 51:17, NASB).

Dave Busby spoke at a Network Forum on Psalm 51: "When God sees a broken heart, one that is yielded to Him, He 'does not despise.' He is attracted. He is drawn to a broken spirit and a yielded heart because they indicate vulnerability. When we are vulnerable, we allow God to mold us. By giving Him access to the innermost workings of our hearts we free Him to do great things in and through us."[31]

So often we are in a hurry. It's not a bad motive. We want to serve God, meet needs, and accomplish our goals. We want to "redeem the time" (Ephesians 5:16). Think of how the disciples (the first network!) felt after Jesus' last words about being His witnesses to all the world. If I had been there, I may have enthusiastically charged off in all directions! I would have already forgotten the first thing Jesus said, "Do not leave Jerusalem, but wait for the gift [the Holy Spirit] . . . " (Acts 1:4-8). Scripture tells us they went directly to the Upper Room and were seemingly prepared to wait indefinitely.

Almost from the beginning of the Network, some of us wanted to do a national conference to impart the vision of networking our efforts to reach and disciple young people. Everyone was positive, but an early decision by the board delayed it for lack of manpower and funds (see chapter 2). A few years later after the Network had grown, we were talking about it again. People were feeling that the time was right so we had begun doing some preliminary work.

Dave Busby was on the board then. We were brainstorming and laying plans, enthusiastic about the idea and how God could use it to further the cause of reaching kids. Just before we were ready to take a vote, Dave interjected, "I have a check in my spirit. I don't feel negative, but I feel we should put this on hold until morning – pray and think about it overnight." Some felt a slight sense of surprise, a little like someone had unexpectedly tapped the brakes. But we all agreed to wait. The board never moved forward without consensus.

After a short discussion the next morning and with little debate or explanation, we all shared a settled conviction that we should wait – again. It may happen someday, but the timing was not yet right. We prayed and moved on to the next agenda item.

What we know now, in hindsight, was that the conference we had been envisioning was the Atlanta 96 Youth Leaders Conference – 8,000 youth workers, co-sponsored by thirty-six other ministries, involving many denominations, 182 exhibitors, and a contingent of 10,000 students. We had no idea what the Lord had in mind, how it would impact the cause of networking to reach youth, and all the other tangent blessings for so many. Waiting was good. God's timing is perfect.

Psalm 78 has always been one of my favorite Scripture passages because it speaks of our need to "tell the next generation the praiseworthy deeds of the Lord . . . even the children yet to be born" (vv. 4, 6). These verses from Psalm 78 are part of my rationale for writing this book. But much of the rest of the chapter is disconcerting because it characterizes the fathers of those generations as stubborn, rebellious, disloyal, and unfaithful (v. 8). As I study the chapter, it repeatedly tells the story that these leaders would not wait on God because "they did not believe in God or trust in His deliverance" (v. 22).

> In our humanity, we are quick to forget the powerful Partner we have!

Why would this be the case after His abundant provision and protection? Simply because they "forgot what he had done, the wonders he had shown them" (v. 11, also v. 42). So that's why Psalm 78 begins with the call to praise and remembrance. It's not just a formality; it is instrumental in helping us yield to God and the leading of His Spirit because, in our humanity, we are so quick to forget the powerful Partner we have!

Be Prepared for the Enemy's Resistance

Seattle was the site of the 1990 Goodwill Games. The ministries of Youth With a Mission and Network Northwest agreed to make it a ministry event, joining together to carry the "eternal" flame throughout the Northwest. They provided students to run from four cities, joining others who had relayed the torch first lit in Israel and converging in Seattle.

Along the way a truck slammed into a support vehicle, slightly injuring two of the runners, and the eternal flame went out! But the greatest resistance took place on the final day at Volunteer Park in Seattle. A day meant for celebration and praise with the teams' families and friends was interrupted by a sizable group arriving to protest the Christian worship and speakers. Tension mounted. The protesters tried to take over the microphone, taunting and interrupting to the point that police showed up in force, fearing a potential riot.

All the while there was prayer. Chris Renzelman, Regional Coordinator of Network Northwest, helped the kids break into small groups to pray for wisdom, protection, unity, and peace. God moved. Confrontation subsided as some of the most verbal protesters began leaving. The small prayer groups were a target for the protesters, but when they tried to interrupt, it turned into positive interaction between the two groups. What was intended for harm, God used for good (Genesis 50:20)!

> *"Be alert and of sober mind. Your enemy the devil prowls around like a roaring lion looking for someone to devour. Resist him, standing firm in the faith..."*
> *(1 Peter 5:8-9).*

Satan is the enemy of unity. His strategy is to stir up unrest and incite division (1 Corinthians 1:10-13, 11:18). If you are no threat to him, he will leave you alone. But take heart if you are undergoing some resistance. It's actually a good sign, for as bomber pilots are known to say, "If you're catching flak, then you're right over the target."

"If you're catching flak, then you're right over the target."

Of course, in ourselves, we are no match for Satan. The good news is found in James 4:7 which says if we submit to God and resist the devil, "he will flee from you." In the verse above, Satan is compared to a roaring lion. My wife and I went on a safari in Africa. Though staying in a well-fenced camp, we could clearly hear the lions' roars. The roar of a male lion is said to carry for about five miles, declaring his ownership of the territory for all who hear. No matter if the lion is young and hearty or old and toothless, his roar is meant to instill fear in any potential aggressors.

Because of our safety within the protective "fence" that the Holy Spirit provides, Satan's only power in the believer's life is what we give him due to fear and lack of submitting to God. But that doesn't mean it's not a battle. When we were leading Atlanta 96, we had so many instances of resistance that we started listing them on our whiteboard as "Roaring Lions"! It helped us to "stand firm in the faith" and not fear his threat.

It seemed that the typical pattern for Satan's work was to create chaos and a flurry of activity and confusion. In our conferences we've had a hotel fire, phone systems go down, and program vendors not show. There have been outages of city power, computer power, and manpower. We've had leaders threatened, speakers cancel, and staff collapse. I don't credit Satan with all that, but I can say, in every situation, that the ensuing stress and chaos was overcome by the Spirit-empowered unity of those who prayed and worked together. When the world sees us experiencing unity and the "peace of God" (Philippians 4:6-7), I believe that is the supernatural impact of what Jesus meant when He talked about causing the world to believe (John 17:21).

Let the Spirit Guide You to Think Outside the Box

When we trust in ourselves, we get what man can do. When we walk in the Spirit, we get what God can do (Psalm 56:3-4).

Jesus' promise of the Holy Spirit changes everything. We all have apprehensions, fears, doubts – whatever you call them. In John 14 I think the disciples were feeling insecure and confused about Jesus returning to His Father. Jesus assured them that if they walked in faith " . . . the works that I do he will do also; and greater works than these he will do" (v. 12). If each of us is walking in that kind of spiritual power, we have every reason to think outside the box.

Richard Ross is a professor of student ministry at Southwestern

> When we trust in ourselves, we get what man can do. When we walk in the Spirit, we get what God can do.

Seminary in Fort Worth, Texas. This gifted leader, who inspired the "True Love Waits" movement, has been a faithful networker for years. Because of his walk in the Spirit, he was open to thinking outside the box about those with whom he networked. He comes regularly to our Youth Ministry Executive Council (YMEC) where he meets with fellow leaders of other denominational youth ministries – a rare opportunity for most of them. Richard shares:

> YMEC introduced me to God's broader family. For example, at one YMEC meeting I was paired with the Assemblies of God leader. His stream of the church was one of those historically viewed with skepticism by my stream. But as we shared and prayed together, I made a remarkable discovery. He had a love for Jesus like mine. And he had a love for teenagers like mine. And he had a strategy for impacting them through the church like mine. My worldview literally changed as I said to myself, "I bet the DNA I share with this man I share with most of the fifty others in this room, including those who represent denominations and groups I once thought were strange!"

Because of Richard's openness to the Spirit's leading, working with others outside the box of "his stream" has accelerated the cause of Christ among young people.

We are not "better together" just because we are uniting with others. Any secular business can do that. Believers who are empowered by the Holy Spirit are better together because we are united with Jesus and God the Father (John 17:21-23). Jeremiah 33:3 conveys God's very words—when His people call upon Him, He will answer them, showing them great things (literally, "unfathomable") that are so outside the box it is beyond our imagination (Ephesians 3:20).

So, we have no need to be intimidated by the size of the task. Throughout the ages, God has used ordinary people to accomplish His will as they yielded their humble means to Him:

> Throughout the ages, God has used ordinary people to accomplish His will as they yielded their humble means to Him.

- Elijah – "A man just like us" whose prayers affected the weather for three and a half years (James 5: 17-18).
- Moses – Transformed from an unconfident speaker (Exodus 4:10) to a bold leader (Hebrews 11:24-29).
- Noah – Who did everything just as God commanded him (Genesis 6:22).
- Abraham – Who went where God told him (Genesis 12:1-4).
- Gideon – Who came from the smallest tribe yet was empowered to save Israel from Midian (Judges 6:11-16).
- Paul – Who was transformed in an instant and obeyed what Jesus told him to do (Acts 9).

The same Holy Spirit who "was hovering over the waters" in Genesis 1:2 lives in you today if you are a believer. The Spirit will work through you in the same way as He has worked in the lives of countless others who yielded to the Spirit's power. As you unite with others in your community, ask the Holy Spirit, who "hovers" there too, to reveal to you what needs exist, what resources are available, and what actions should be taken for the glory of God.

We are "Better Together!"

I was sharing with my adult son, Tyler, about a difficulty I was facing. Having learned much from his own challenges in life, he looked at me lovingly and said, "Dad, remember, it's not all about you!" Tyler instantly broadened my perspective as I thought about God's will and bigger purpose in my life. Unity is not all about us. It is about the mission that God has called us to. And that mission, to go to all the world starting with our Jerusalem, demands unity with others – but "not by might or by power but by My Spirit says the Lord" (Zechariah 4:6).

"Better Together" Questions

1. Are you confident that you are personally empowered by the Holy Spirit right now? If not, take some time to 1) confess any known sin and 2) surrender to the Spirit's control.

2. The leaders of Israel struggled to trust God because they kept forgetting what He had already done to encourage their faith. Consider making a list of some of the things God has done in your network. What things stand out that increase your faith for the issues you currently face?

3. What are the "roaring lions" you are experiencing now (or recently) where Satan is trying to instill fear and hinder you?

4. As you think of the Holy Spirit hovering over your community, what do you think stands out? What needs exist? What resources are available? What actions should you take?

Better Together demonstrates its thesis through a coalition of ministries committed to "the dynamic results of cooperation." We thank each of these sponsors for their commitment to making this resource a part of their approach to training and encouraging their constituencies. May God multiply the future use of these principles far and wide!

"Better Together" Book Sponsors

Organization	Website	Address	City/State/Zip
Assemblies of God/Youth Alive	www.ag.org	1445 Booneville Avenue	Springfield, MO 65802
Christian Educators Association International	www.ceai.org	PO Box 45610	Westlake, OH 44145
Christ for Native Youth	www.nativeyouth.com	PO Box 67677	Albuquerque, NM 87193
Cru (Campus Crusade for Christ)	www.cru.org	100 Lake Hart Drive	Orlando, FL 32832
Fellowship of Christian Athletes	www.fca.org	8701 Leeds Road	Kansas City, MO 64129
Group Magazine/Simply Youth	www.group.com	1515 Cascade Avenue	Loveland, CO 80538
Josh McDowell Ministry	www.Josh.org	2001 W. Plano Parkway, Suite 2400	Plano, TX 75075
National Network of Youth Ministries	www.nnym.org	PO Box 501748	San Diego, CA 92150
One Hope International	www.onehope.net	600 SW Third Street	Pompano Beach, FL 33060
Reach Out Youth Solutions	www.reach-out.org	PO Box 870141	Stone Mountain, GA 30087
Student Discipleship Ministries	www.gosdm.org	PO Box 6747	Fort Worth, TX 76115
Teen Mania	www.teenmania.org	PO Box 2000	Garden Valley, TX 75771
The Great Commission Coalition	www.greatcommissioncoalition.com	PO Box 6787	Kingwood, TX 77325
Urban Youth Worker Institute	www.uywi.org	2321 E. 4th Street, Suite C607	Santa Ana, CA 92705
Vineyard Churches	www.vineyardotr.org	1201 Riverside Ave.	Fort Collins, CO 80524
Youth for Christ/USA	www.yfc.net	PO Box 4478	Englewood, CO 80155
Youth Ministry International	www.ymitraining.com	1300 Envoy Circle, Ste 1306	Louisville, KY 40299
Youth Specialties	www.youthspecialties.com	PO Box 166317	Irving, TX 75016
Youth Unlimited	www.youthunlimited.org	PO Box 7259	Grand Rapids, MI 49510
Youth With a Mission	www.usrenewal.org	PO Box 1634	Port Orchard, WA 98366

APPENDIX 1

The Network Covenant is a core document of the National Network of Youth Ministries. The statement below was signed by the founders in 1981 and by individual Network members in the ensuing years. The current edition of the covenant can be found at www.youthworkers.net.

Network Covenant

"Constrained by the love of Christ,"
motivated by a love for young people,
and empowered by the indwelling Holy Spirit,
I hereby enter into a covenant with God
and with my co-laborers in youth ministry.
I claim by faith that my life will be characterized by:

PERSONAL HOLINESS before God and others, which is established in Christ and expressed in daily life through prayer and commitment to the Word of God.

AN EXEMPLARY HOME LIFE which is a source of renewal for me and my family and a godly model for others to follow.

A LIFE OF DISCIPLESHIP which is reproducing an on-going chain of maturing believers.

INVOLVEMENT IN EVANGELISM which helps expose every teenager to the gospel in a personal and culturally relevant way.

A WILLINGNESS TO MINISTER TO YOUTH FOR A LIFETIME, should God so direct.

A MINISTRY WHICH BECOMES A RESOURCE to other churches and organizations, cooperating with others for greater effectiveness in ministering to teenagers.

I solemnly establish this covenant on this _____ day of
_____, _____

Signature _____

APPENDIX 2

The Challenge 2000 Pledge

originally issued at the Atlanta 96 Youth Leaders Conference.

CHALLENGE 2000

BECAUSE JESUS LOVES ME AND I LOVE HIM, I WILL:

COMMIT myself to a love relationship with Jesus Christ . . . through praying, studying His Word, and allowing His Spirit to lead me each day.

Matthew 22:36-38

HONOR Christ in my moral life . . . my thoughts, words, actions and relationships.

1 Timothy 4:12

RESPECT my parents and all authorities in my life . . . with love, honor and obedience.

Ephesians 6:1-3, Romans 13:1

INVEST myself in encouraging and uniting with other Christians . . . regardless of race, church or social status.

Hebrews 10:24-25

SEEK God through prayer . . . asking Him daily to bring spiritual awakening to my generation.

2 Chronicles 7:14

TAKE the message of Christ to my school and world . . . by praying, living and witnessing so that every student has the opportunity to know Christ.

Acts 1:8

BELIEVING GOD HAS A SPECIAL DESTINY AND MISSION FOR ME AND MY GENERATION, I TAKE THIS CHALLENGE, RELYING ON THE HOLY SPIRIT.

I join young people and youth workers around the world to pray for a spiritual awakening, and to help take the message of Christ to every school and every young person by the year 2000.

Signed _____

Date _____

Challenge 2000 is a cooperative effort by Christian denominations and youth organizations and is coordinated by the National Network of Youth Ministries.

APPENDIX 3

A Healthy Ministry Network includes . . .

A community of youth workers, students and caring adults who unite by praying together and sharing relationships, resources, and strategy to reach and equip teenagers for Christ.

>PRAY
TOGETHER
Discover God's DNA for
your community.

+ Connect through prayer.
+ Ask God for His vision.
+ Establish a foundation of prayer.
+ Pray in three dimensions.

>BUILD
RELATIONSHIPS
Build a team that does life
and ministry together.

+ Develop trust.
+ Gather your core team.
+ Meet together for nurture and
  equipping.
+ Establish common ground.

HEALTHY MINISTRY NETWORK

>DEVELOP
STRATEGIES
Make plans to mobilize
youth and adults in your
community.

+ Create an Action Plan:
+ Discover
+ Design
+ Do

>SHARE
RESOURCES
Utilize the assets God
provides for your community.

+ Recruit more workers.
+ Widen the net.
+ Serve in your strengths.
+ Evaluate, adjust and stay
  in the game.

APPENDIX 4

Partphering Continuum

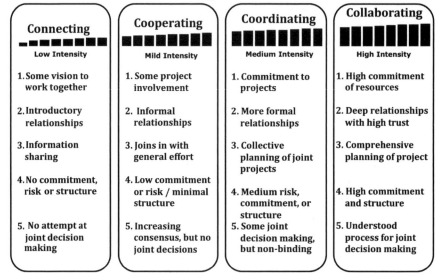

Connecting	**Cooperating**	**Coordinating**	**Collaborating**
Low Intensity	Mild Intensity	Medium Intensity	High Intensity
1. Some vision to work together	1. Some project involvement	1. Commitment to projects	1. High commitment of resources
2. Introductory relationships	2. Informal relationships	2. More formal relationships	2. Deep relationships with high trust
3. Information sharing	3. Joins in with general effort	3. Collective planning of joint projects	3. Comprehensive planning of project
4. No commitment, risk or structure	4. Low commitment or risk / minimal structure	4. Medium risk, commitment, or structure	4. High commitment and structure
5. No attempt at joint decision making	5. Increasing consensus, but no joint decisions	5. Some joint decision making, but non-binding	5. Understood process for joint decision making

ENDNOTES

Foreword

[1] Mike Kilen, "Community Rallies When Girl Wanders into Cornfield," *Des Moines Register* (July 7, 2012): http://www.*Des Moines Register*.com.

Chapter 1: Passionate Vision

[2] Roger Randall, Letter (October 4, 2012).

[3] Rick Warren, "Reigniting Your Passion for God" (July, 2003): http://www.sermoncentral.com.

[4] U.S. Census Bureau, ACS Demographic and Housing Estimates (2008-2012).

[5] Oswald Chambers, *My Utmost for His Highest* (New York: Dodd, Mead and Co., 1954), 188.

Chapter 3: Shared Purpose

[6] Mark Ross, "In Essentials Unity, In Non-Essentials Liberty, In All Things Charity," *Tabletalk* Magazine, Ligonier Blog (September 16, 2009): http://www.ligonier.org.

Chapter 5: Mutual Trust

[7] Michael Hyatt, "Episode 1: The Five Benefits of Collaboration," Podcast, (July 9, 2014): http://www.Michaelhyatt.com.

[8] Billy Beacham, "Unpacking the DNA of the Network," *Network Magazine*, Vol. 24, No. 2 (Summer, 2006), 23.

Chapter 6: Big Dreams

[9] Dan Graves, "The Deathless Sermon," *The Trumpet Newsletter,* New Testament Christian Church's online monthly newsletter (August 10, 2012): http://www.ntccgoodnews.com/?p=2814.

[10] "William Carey," *Wikipedia,* Justo L. Gonzalez, *The Story of Christianity,* Vol. 2 (Harperone: 2010), 306.

[11] Jim Rayburn, "The Big Dream," Address to Young Life staff, 1970 (February 6, 2014): https://www.youtube.com/watch?v=tLxDQOtXNzc.

[12] Richard Baxter, "The Need for Unity and Fellowship Among Pastors," *Network Magazine,* (Summer, 2006), 18.

[13] "Challenge 2000 Market Research Study," (Integrity Marketing Group: March 17, 2000).

[14] "Campus Alliance," http://www.Everyschool.com.

Chapter 7: Leverage Resources

[15] Hyatt, "Episode 1."

[16] Beacham, "Unpacking the DNA," 24.

Chapter 8: United Prayer

[17] Jonathon Edwards, *A Call to United, Extraordinary Prayer,* Reprint (Ross-shire, Great Britain: Christian Heritage, 2003), 24.

[18] "See You at the Pole," Public Statement (Barna Research Group: September, 1993).

[19] Bryant, David, "The Most Hopeful Sign of Our Times," (Wheaton, IL: The Forerunner, March 31, 2008), http://www.forerunner.com.

Chapter 9: Connected Gatekeepers

[20] Steve Douglass, *Connection* (Orlando, FL: Cru Staff Newsletter, December, 2013), 1.

[21] Wesley Duewel, *Mighty Prevailing Prayer,* (Grand Rapids, MI: Zondervan), 129ff.

Chapter 10: Grassroots Impact

[22] "A Ministry to Every Campus," 1987 Progress Report, NNYM Forum '88, Program, 11.

[23] Speech delivered at Network Banquet, San Diego, October 1993.

[24] Phill Butler, *Well Connected* (Waynesboro, GA: Authentic Media, 2005), 16.

[25] Ibid, 16, 196.

[26] *The Next Mile*, (Delta Ministries, 2006): http://www.thenextmile.org.

Chapter 12: Spirit-empowered Unity

[27] Max Lucado, "All by Myself," *365 Inspirational Spots*, Audio blog, September 4, 2013.

[28] William R. Bright, "Have you made the Wonderful Discovery of the Spirit-Filled Life?" (Cru, 2008).

[29] Spirit of Revival, *Bend the Church and Save the World*, Vol. 18, No. 1 (Buchanan, Michigan: Life Action Ministries),18.

[30] A. W. Tozer, *The Pursuit of God* (Harrisburg, PA: Christian Publications, 1948). 97.

[31] Dave Busby, *Network News*, Editorial, Vol. 5, No. 1 (Winter, 1987), 3.

BIBLIOGRAPHY

Baxter, Richard. "The Need for Unity and Fellowship Among Pastors," *Network Magazine,* Summer, 2006.

Beacham, Billy. "Unpacking the DNA of the Network." <u>Network Magazine,</u> Vol. 24, No. 2. Summer, 2006.

Bright, William R. "Have you made the Wonderful Discovery of the Spirit-Filled Life?" Cru, 2008.

Bryant, David, "The Most Hopeful Sign of Our Times," Wheaton, IL: The Forerunner (March 31, 2008): http://www.forerunner.com.

Busby, Dave. *Network News,* Editorial, Vol. 5, No. 1. Winter, 1987.

Butler, Phill. *Well Connected.* Waynesboro, GA: Authentic Media, 2005.

"Challenge 2000 Market Research Study," Integrity Marketing Group, March 17, 2000.

Chambers, Oswald. *My Utmost for His Highest.* New York: Dodd, Mead and Co., 1954.

Douglass, Steven. *Connection.* Orlando, FL: Cru Staff Newsletter, December, 2013.

Duewel, Wesley. *Mighty Prevailing Prayer.* Grand Rapids, MI: Zondervan, 1990.

Edwards, Jonathon. *A Call to United, Extraordinary Prayer,* Reprint. Ross-shire, Great Britain: Christian Heritage, 2003.

Graves, Dan. "The Deathless Sermon." *The Trumpet Newsletter.* New Testament Christian Church's online monthly newsletter. (August 10, 2012): http://www.ntccgoodnews.com/?p=2814.

Hyatt, Michael. "Episode 1: The Five Benefits of Collaboration," Podcast. (July 9, 2014): http://www.Michaelhyatt.com.

Kilen, Mike. "Community Rallies When Girl Wanders into Cornfield." *Des Moines Register* (July 7, 2012): http://www.*Des Moines Register*.com.

Lucado, Max. "All by Myself," *365 Inspirational Spots*, Audio blog. September 4, 2013.

"A Ministry to Every Campus." 1987 Progress Report. NNYM Forum '88 Program.

The Next Mile. Delta Ministries (2006): http://www.thenextmile.org.

Randall, Roger. Letter. October 4, 2012.

Rayburn, Jim. "The Big Dream." Address to Young Life staff, 1970. (February 6, 2014): https://www.youtube.com/watch?v=tLxDQOtXNzc.

Ross, Mark. "In Essentials Unity, In Non-Essentials Liberty, In All Things Charity." *Tabletalk* Magazine, Ligonier Blog (September 16, 2009): http://www.ligonier.org.

See You at the Pole. Public Statement. Barna Research Group, September, 1993.

Speech by Jim Burns delivered at Network Banquet. San Diego. October, 1993.

Spirit of Revival. *Bend the Church and Save the World.* Vol. 18, No. 1, Buchanan, Michigan: Life Action Ministries.

Tozer, A. W. *The Pursuit of God.* Harrisburg, Pennsylvania: Christian Publications, 1948.

U.S. Census Bureau. ACS Demographic and Housing Estimates. 2008-2012.

Warren, Rick. "Reigniting Your Passion for God." (July, 2003): http://www.sermoncentral.com.

"William Carey." *Wikipedia.* Justo L. Gonzalez, *The Story of Christianity,* Vol. 2, Harperone: 2010.

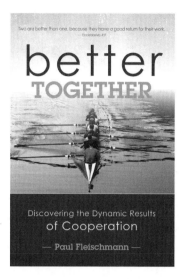

IF YOU'RE A FAN OF
BETTER TOGETHER,
PLEASE TELL OTHERS

Write a positive review on www.amazon.com.

Purchase additional copies to give away as gifts.

Suggest *Better Together* to friends.

Write about *Better Together* on your blog.

Post excerpts to your social media sites
such as: Facebook, Twitter, Pinterest, Instagram, etc.

When you're in a bookstore, ask if they carry the book. The book is
available through all major distributors, so any bookstore that does not
have it in stock can easily order it.

Order additional copies of *Better Together* from your local bookstore or by
going to the Network website: www.nnym.org.
Inquire about special quantity discounts.

aRE YOU COnnECTED?

"My friends, life is about relationships. The more I speak with youth workers, the greater
the need I see for them to connect with others like themselves. I'm surprised at how
unconnected some youth workers are! You need to get networked and connected."

       - Doug Fields, NNYM member, youth ministry author and speaker

Better Together
Do you feel alone in youth ministry?

Youth leaders who do life and ministry together reach teenagers more effectively, model unity, and last
longer in ministry. Collaboration leads to a greater impact in their community.

Four Priorities
That's what the National Network of
Youth Ministries is all about. All over the
U.S., healthy ministry networks of youth
leaders, students, and caring adults are
uniting around four priorities:

>PRAY TOGETHER

>BUILD RELATIONSHIPS

HEALTHY MINISTRY NETWORK

Why Network?
The Network connects you with people
for encouragement, spiritual growth and
sharing resources to reach and empower
teenagers. We value:

>DEVELOP STRATEGIES

>SHARE RESOURCES

+ Personal discipleship.
+ Equipping students.
+ Sharing the gospel.
+ Collaborative partnerships.

We Invite You To Join Us

Go to youthworkers.net/networks and
  + Register for free.
  + Connect with a local network.
  + Start/list a network in your community.

Find us online at
  + web: youthworkers.net
  + twitter: @nnym
  + facebook: nationalnetwork

NNYM
National Network of Youth Ministries

PO BOX 501748 - San Diego, CA 92150 (858) 451-1111

Building a ministry network
that brings hope to youth
in your community.

Want to start a ministry network?

NNYM can help!

Visit youthworkers.net/training to get started.